The Singer's Daily Practice Journal

Volume I: A graded introduction to vocal technique and diction

Cheri Montgomery

S.T.M. Publishers
Nashville, TN

Copies of this book may be ordered by contacting:

S.T.M. Publishers
P.O. Box 111485, Nashville, TN 37222
Tel: (615) 831-9859 Fax: (615) 831-7148
Email: info@studenttextmfg.com
Website: www.stmpublishers.com
Facebook: *Lyric Diction Workbook Series*

The Singer's Daily Practice Journal, volume I, student manual
ISBN 978-1-7352114-0-4

Student manuals for voice and diction from S.T.M. Publishers:

ISBN 978-1-7338631-0-0	Singer's Diction
ISBN 978-1-7352114-0-4	The Singer's Daily Practice Journal, volume I
ISBN 978-0-9975578-7-9	The Singer's Daily Practice Journal, volume II
ISBN 978-1-7338631-6-2	The Singer's Daily Practice Journal, volume III
ISBN 978-1-7338631-2-4	IPA Handbook for Singers, 2nd edition
ISBN 978-0-9975578-3-1	Phonetic Readings for Lyric Diction, 3rd edition
ISBN 978-0-9975578-0-0	Phonetic Transcription for Lyric Diction
ISBN 978-0-9975578-5-5	Phonetic Transcription for Lyric Diction, expanded
ISBN 978-1-7338631-5-5	English Lyric Diction Workbook, 4th ed.
ISBN 978-0-9818829-8-7	Italian Lyric Diction Workbook, 3rd edition
ISBN 978-0-9916559-2-2	Latin Lyric Diction Workbook
ISBN 978-0-9818829-6-3	German Lyric Diction Workbook, 5th edition
ISBN 978-0-9916559-1-5	French Lyric Diction Workbook, 4th edition
ISBN 978-0-9916559-5-3	Advanced French Lyric Diction Workbook
ISBN 978-1-7352114-4-2	Russian Lyric Diction Workbook
ISBN 978-1-7352114-9-7	Spanish Lyric Diction Workbook

Technical Support: Verlan Kliewer

To: Brenna Rae Montgomery

Acknowledgements

I've been blessed to work with excellent mentors. First of whom is my father, Archie Kliewer. His love for singing, diction, and vocal pedagogy inspired the many teachers and singers he met as Regional Governor of NATS and Professor of Voice at Belmont University and Southern Seminary, Louisville. I treasure our many conversations about voice and diction. Recalling his words of wisdom keep his memory close. He advised: "Most of what you need to become a good teacher will be gained on the job". How true! My love for teaching and desire to find a cohesive pedagogy grew out of my work with private voice students and the diction courses. These experiences helped me discover a practical application of diction as it relates to the process of singing. My voice teacher, George Bitzas, Professor of Voice at the University of Tennessee, Knoxville, was a wise and careful mentor. I am thankful for the time I had to work with him and for his insistence on legato and beautiful singing.

I owe special thanks to Dr. Katherine Jolly, Assistant Professor at the Indiana University Jacobs School of Music, for the lovely images. She perfectly embodies the singer's facial structure and stance. Her willingness to model the many vowel and consonant formations is much appreciated.

Verlan Kliewer's programing skills greatly simplified the transcription process. I am grateful for his patient assistance.

Cheri Montgomery
Author and Lecturer
Blair School of Music at
Vanderbilt University

Preface

Students would benefit from daily lessons in the first year of study. There are many skills to be acquired at once and much of the information must be tailored to match the student's unique ability. This planner provides general information about the singing process and includes daily written assignments. The goal is to keep the singer thinking about their lessons throughout the week and to give the instructor an additional way of assessing the student's level of commitment. A sample voice syllabus and gradebook are available on the instructor's page at www.stmpublishers.com.

The *International Phonetic Alphabet* (IPA) gives the teacher a means of communicating precise sounds for vocal exercises and literature assignments. The vocal apparatus is uniquely structured for language. The sounds of language are uniquely suited for the vocal instrument. Consonants and vowels help us understand the function of the voice. They are useful for training, building, and refining the voice. Vocal concepts in this text are discussed using the IPA. The symbols selected represent an elegant manner of pronunciation as recommended by Madeleine Marshall, author of *The Singer's Manual of English Diction*. Space is provided beneath the IPA for students to supply the English translation. This approach gives students the opportunity to hear proper English and to complete a daily written assignment.

All three volumes in this series combine textbook, workbook, and journal in one resource for voice students. The exercises, written in the treble clef, are to be transposed an octave lower for the male voice. Each section of the 15-week journal begins with manuscript paper for recording weekly lesson notes, exercises, and assignments. A check-list of vocal concepts is included. This gives the teacher the ability to direct students to the precise concept (with lesson and page number) that requires attention for the week. The following page provides space for the student to record progress and log daily practice times.

Preface (continued)

The Singers Daily Practice Journal prepares the student for English, Italian, German, French, and Latin repertoire assignments by providing a graded introduction to phonetic transcription, phonetic reading, and classical singing technique.

An abbreviated version of the pedagogy within this text is published in the *Journal of Singing*, Jan./Feb. 2018 issue: *The Voice and Diction Connection, A Diction Instructor's Approach to Voice Pedagogy* by Cheri Montgomery.

CM

Table of Contents

Table of Contents

Table of Contents

English Transcription: Week 1

Day 1: Introduction to the IPA

Day 2: English Front Vowels

Day 3: English Back Vowels

Day 4: English Central Vowels

Day 5: English Consonants – Fricatives

Day 6: English Consonants – Affricates,
       [j] Glide, and Nasal [ŋ]

Lesson Notes, Date: _________

Checklist of Concepts to Review

BREATH
Breath Control___
p: 35, 63, 67
Breath Support___
p: 63, 65
Breath Expansion___
p: 33, 35
DICTION
Articulation___
p: 121, 123, 125, 131
Front Vowels___
p: 57, 105
Back Vowels___
p: 73, 107
Central Vowels___
p: 89, 91, 93, 109, 111
Mixed Vowels___
p: 113, 115
FLEXIBILITY
Flexibility___
p: 109, 139
MUSICIANSHIP
Artistry___
p: 141
Dynamics___
p: 143
Legato___
p: 49, 59, 75, 139, 141

POSTURE
Postural Alignment___
p: 25, 27
RANGE
Range___
p: 81, 91, 139
TONE
Chiaroscuro___
p: 97, 113, 115
Lip Trills___
p: 41, 43
Palatal Resonance___
p: 89, 91, 93, 109
Pharyngeal Space___
p: 57, 59, 93, 105, 109
Projection___
p: 73, 75, 93, 107
Register___
p: 43, 83
Resonance___
p: 93, 95, 97, 109, 137
Sensory Awareness___
p: 61, 127
Vibrato___
p: 43, 45, 51, 77, 79, 81
Vowel Equalization___
p: 79, 95, 137
WARM-UPS___
p: 200-204

WARNINGS
Breathy Tone___
p: 35, 77, 113, 125, 127
Faulty Formation___
p. 111, 127
Faulty Movement___
p. 45, 47
Faulty Onset___
p: 59, 75, 127
Jaw Tension___
p: 31, 111, 121, 123, 125
Nasal Tone ___
p: 111, 127
Pressed Tone___
p: 35, 41, 43, 83
Spread Tone___
p: 57, 61, 73, 111
Tension___
p: 29, 31, 45, 47, 61
Tongue Impeded Tone__
p: 111, 127
OTHER
Choral Singing___
p: 99
Stage Deportment___
p: 145
Vocal health___
p: 147

Daily Notes and Practice Times

Day 1   Practice Time:___________

Day 2   Practice Time:___________

Day 3   Practice Time:___________

Day 4   Practice Time:___________

Day 5   Practice Time:___________

Day 6   Practice Time:___________

The International Phonetic Alphabet

The IPA was established by the International Phonetic Association around 1888. Each symbol stands for one sound. Brackets enclose the symbols of a word or phrase. Precise pronunciation of each symbol must be defined within the respective language. Vowel and consonant terms are defined on pages 152 and 153.

English Transcription

Silent vowels are not transcribed. A final *e* is often silent in English. For example, the four-letter word *love* [lʌv] is transcribed with three symbols to represent the three sounds that are actually pronounced. Single vowels may have more than one sound. The *i* of *like* [lɑːɪk] is transcribed with two symbols to represent the two sounds pronounced. Sometimes a vowel cluster makes one sound as in the word *tree* [tɹi]. Silent consonants are not transcribed. The *l* of *could* [kʊd] is silent. Double consonants are represented with a single symbol as in the word *call* [kɔl]. Some consonants have phonetic changes. Pronunciation depends on the consonant's position within the word. For example, a final *s* is [z] when proceeded by a voiced consonant: *waves* [wɛːɪvz]. A final *d* is [t] when proceeded by a voiceless consonant: *looked* [lʊkt].

Here is a list of IPA symbols with common English spellings:

[ɑ]: *a, o*	[h]: *h*	[o]: *o*	[u]: *oo, ou, u, ew*
[æ]: *a*	[i]: *ee, ea, ie*	[ɔ]: *al, aw, or, au, ou*	[ʊ]: *oo, ou, u*
[b]: *b*	[ɪ]: *i, ie, ui, y*	[p]: *p*	[ʌ]: *o, u, ou*
[d]: *d, t*	[j]: *y*	[ɹ] and [r]: *r*	[v]: *v*
[ɛ]: *e, ea, ie, ai*	[k]: *c, ck, qu*	[s]: *c, s*	[w]: *w*
[ɜ]: vowel + *r*	[ks]: *x*	[ʃ]: *sh, ch*	[ʍ]: *wh*
[f]: *f, ph, gh*	[l]: *l*	[t]: *t*	[z]: *z, s*
[g]: *g*	[m]: *m*	[tʃ]: *ch*	[ʒ]: *z, s*
[dʒ]: *g, j*	[n]: *n*	[ð]: *th*	[']: stress mark
[gz]: *x*	[ŋ]: *ng, nk*	[θ]: *th*	[:]: long mark

The schwa [ə] stands for an undefined sound in an unstressed syllable. It has many sounds in English. Pronunciation is based on spelling and duration of the note. For example, the *e* of *golden* is pronounced as an [ɪ] sound when set on a short note. It is [ɛ] when set on a sustained tone. The pronunciation of vowels in unstressed syllables is defined in this text according to the sustained pronunciation. Note: The sound of unstressed [æ] is often mixed with [ɪ] or [ʌ]: *fountain* [ˈfɑːʊntæn].

English Front Vowels

IPA	English	Transcription	Rules
[i]	sea	[si]	*e, ee, ea, ie, eo* spellings
[ɪ]	fit	[fɪt]	*i, ie, ui, y* spellings
[ɛ]	bells	[bɛlz]	*e, ea, ie, ai* spellings
[s]	scent	[sɛnt]	*c* + front vowel
[k]	clear	[klɪːʌ]	*c* + back vowel or consonant

Provide IPA:

1. keys	twelve	picked	weeps
2. fence	kissed	speaks	quick
3. minced	peaks	elms	knees
4. cleansed	fixed	queen	guessed
5. limbs	dwells	his	zeal
6. helped	gives	ceased	debts

Provide English Spelling:

1. [ɛls]	[pis]	[bɪlt]	[hɛns]
2. [sinz]	[nɛkst]	[ist]	[klɪk]
3. [hɪmz]	[sɪns]	[kwɛst]	[gis]

Answer Key:

1. [kiz]	[twɛlv]	[pɪkt]	[wips]
2. [fɛns]	[kɪst]	[spiks]	[kwɪk]
3. [mɪnst]	[piks]	[ɛlmz]	[niz]
4. [klɛnzd]	[fɪkst]	[kwin]	[gɛst]
5. [lɪmz]	[dwɛlz]	[hɪz]	[zil]
6. [hɛlpt]	[gɪvz]	[sist]	[dɛts]
1. else	peace	built	hence
2. scenes	next	east	click
3. hymns	since	quest	geese

English Back Vowels

IPA	English	Transcription	Rules
[u]	blue	[blu]	*o, oo, ou, u, ew* spellings
[ʊ]	look	[lʊk]	*o, oo, ou, u* spellings
[ɔ]	ought	[ɔt]	*al, aw, or, au, ou, war* spellings

Provide IPA:

1. clue	bought	good	spooks
2. woods	two	hawk	pulled
3. taught	cooks	pools	walk
4. bull	moves	called	nook
5. loosed	fawn	hood	moods
6. stalk	tomb	cause	foot

Provide English Spelling:

1. [wʊlvz]	[kɔt]	[hu]	[stʊd]
2. [fɔt]	[sun]	[kʊd]	[tɔkt]
3. [skul]	[tʊk]	[dɔnz]	[buts]

Answer Key:

1. [klu]	[bɔt]	[gʊd]	[spuks]
2. [wʊdz]	[tu]	[hɔk]	[pʊld]
3. [tɔt]	[kʊks]	[pulz]	[wɔk]
4. [bʊl]	[muvz]	[kɔld]	[nʊk]
5. [lust]	[fɔn]	[hʊd]	[mudz]
6. [stɔk]	[tum]	[kɔz]	[fʊt]

1. wolves	caught	who	stood
2. fought	soon	could	talked
3. school	took	dawns	boots

English Central Vowels

IPA	English	Transcription	Rules
[ɑ]	swan	[swɑn]	*a, o, alm* spellings
[æ]	hat	[hæt]	*a* spelling
[ʌ]	up	[ʌp]	*o, oo, u, ou* spellings
[ɜ]	bird	[bɜd]	vowel + *r*

Provide IPA:

1. wand   sir   cap   tough

2. fact   cut   turn   knock

3. pearls   balm   doves   hands

4. buds   glad   stop   words

5. clock   burns   lamps   sulk

6. back   flood   heard   palms

Provide English Spelling:

1. [gɜl]   [kɑmz]   [nʌm]   [ækts]

2. [æks]   [wʌnz]   [pɑnd]   [wɜ]

3. [wʌns]   [læm]   [fɜst]   [ɑks]

Answer Key:
1. [wɑnd]   [sɜ]   [kæp]   [tʌf]
2. [fækt]   [kʌt]   [tɜn]   [nɑk]
3. [pɜlz]   [bɑm]   [dʌvz]   [hændz]
4. [bʌdz]   [glæd]   [stɑp]   [wɜdz]
5. [klɑk]   [bɜnz]   [læmps]   [sʌlk]
6. [bæk]   [flʌd]   [hɜd]   [pɑmz]
1. girl   calms   numb   acts
2. axe   ones   pond   were
3. once   lamb   first   ox

English Consonants – Fricatives

IPA	English	Transcription	Rules (see p. 62)
[ð]	clothe	[klo:ʊð]	voiced *th*
[θ]	thought	[θɔt]	voiceless *th*
[ʒ]	treasure	[ˈtɹɛʒʊ]	voiced *s, z*
[ʃ]	shell	[ʃɛl]	voiceless *sh, ch*

Provide IPA:

1. sheet   that   visions   doth

2. then   shut   thin   bush

3. azure   thoughts   confusion (*u* [ju])   smooth

4. thief   measures   them   flash

5. division   thus   shoe   thumb

6. these   sheep   cloth   version

Provide English Spelling:

1. [suð]   [ˈplɛʒʊ]   [ʃʊd]   [ðɪs]

2. [ˈkæʒuʊl]   [ðæn]   [θim]   [ʃɔl]

3. [buθ]   [ʃɪps]   [ˈtɹɛʒʊz]   [dɛpθs]

Answer Key:

1. [ʃit]   [ðæt]   [ˈvɪʒʌnz]   [dʌθ]
2. [ðɛn]   [ʃʌt]   [θɪn]   [bʊʃ]
3. [ˈæʒʊ]   [θɔts]   [kʌnˈfjuʒʌn]   [smuð]
4. [θif]   [ˈmɛʒʊz]   [ðɛm]   [flæʃ]
5. [dɪˈvɪʒʌn]   [ðʌs]   [ʃu]   [θʌm]
6. [ðiz]   [ʃip]   [klɑθ]   [ˈvɜʒʌn]

1. soothe   pleasure   should   this
2. casual   than   theme   shawl
3. booth   ships   treasures   depths

English Consonants – Affricates, [j] Glide, and Nasal [ŋ]

IPA	English	Transcription	Rules
[ʤ]	judge	[ʤʌʤ]	*j* and *g* spellings
[ʧ]	chair	[ʧɛːʌ]	*ch* spelling
[j]	year	[jɪːʌ]	*y* spelling; *l, s, t, n, d, th + u/ew*
[ʍ]	wheat	[ʍit]	*wh* spelling
[ŋ]	song	[sɑŋ]	*ng* and *nk* spellings

Provide IPA:

1. wing   yes   when   speech

2. just   watch   tune   whipped

3. touched   sing   edge   young

4. whit   gems   few   cheeks

5. dew   wheel   wink   tinge

6. thank   yield   huge   what

Provide English Spelling:

1. [sjut]   [tʌŋ]   [ʧuz]   [ʍit]

2. [θɪŋz]   [sɪnʤ]   [ʍɪʧ]   [jɛt]

3. [jus]   [ʍɛns]   [bæʤ]   [iʧ]

Answer Key:

1. [wɪŋ]   [jɛs]   [ʍɛn]   [spiʧ]
2. [ʤʌst]   [waʧ]   [tjun]   [ʍɪpt]
3. [tʌʧt]   [sɪŋ]   [ɛʤ]   [jʌŋ]
4. [ʍɪt]   [ʤɛmz]   [fju]   [ʧiks]
5. [dju]   [ʍil]   [wɪŋk]   [tɪnʤ]
6. [θæŋk]   [jild]   [hjuʤ]   [ʍat]

1. suit   tongue   choose   wheat
2. things   singe   which   yet
3. use   whence   badge   each

English Transcription: Week 2

Day 1: Transcription of English "r"

Day 2: English Diphthongs

Day 3: Vowel Replacement of "r"

Day 4: Polysyllabic Words

Day 5: Review of English Transcription Rules

Day 6: Phonetic Reading of English Text

Lesson Notes, Date: _______________

Checklist of Concepts to Review

BREATH
Breath Control___
p: 35, 63, 67
Breath Support___
p: 63, 65
Breath Expansion___
p: 33, 35
DICTION
Articulation___
p: 121, 123, 125, 131
Front Vowels___
p: 57, 105
Back Vowels___
p: 73, 107
Central Vowels___
p: 89, 91, 93, 109, 111
Mixed Vowels___
p: 113, 115
FLEXIBILITY
Flexibility___
p: 109, 139
MUSICIANSHIP
Artistry___
p: 141
Dynamics___
p: 143
Legato___
p: 49, 59, 75, 139, 141

POSTURE
Postural Alignment___
p: 25, 27
RANGE
Range___
p: 81, 91, 139
TONE
Chiaroscuro___
p: 97, 113, 115
Lip Trills___
p: 41, 43
Palatal Resonance___
p: 89, 91, 93, 109
Pharyngeal Space___
p: 57, 59, 93, 105, 109
Projection___
p: 73, 75, 93, 107
Register___
p: 43, 83
Resonance___
p: 93, 95, 97, 109, 137
Sensory Awareness___
p: 61, 127
Vibrato___
p: 43, 45, 51, 77, 79, 81
Vowel Equalization___
p: 79, 95, 137
WARM-UPS___
p: 200-204

WARNINGS
Breathy Tone___
p: 35, 77, 113, 125, 127
Faulty Formation___
p. 111, 127
Faulty Movement___
p. 45, 47
Faulty Onset___
p: 59, 75, 127
Jaw Tension___
p: 31, 111, 121, 123, 125
Nasal Tone ___
p: 111, 127
Pressed Tone___
p: 35, 41, 43, 83
Spread Tone___
p: 57, 61, 73, 111
Tension___
p: 29, 31, 45, 47, 61
Tongue Impeded Tone__
p: 111, 127
OTHER
Choral Singing___
p: 99
Stage Deportment___
p: 145
Vocal health___
p: 147

Daily Notes and Practice Times

Day 1   Practice Time:___________

Day 2   Practice Time:___________

Day 3   Practice Time:___________

Day 4   Practice Time:___________

Day 5   Practice Time:___________

Day 6   Practice Time:___________

Transcription of English "r"

IPA	English	Transcription	Rules
Silent *r*	heart, star	[hɑt], [stɑ]	*r* + consonant; final *r*
Flipped [ɾ]	spirit	[ˈspɪɾɪt]	vowel + *r* + vowel
Flipped [ɾ]	thrill, rue	[θɾɪl], [ɾɾu]	*thr* spelling; *r* + [u]
Flipped [ɾ]	grave	[gɾɛːɪv]	*cr, gr of* dramatic words
Retroflex [ɹ]	dream	[dɹim]	*r* + vowel

Provide IPA:

1.	friends	thread	cherished	guard
2.	parents	green	sword	cross
3.	crushed	warm	fruit	laurels
4.	truth	spring	chorus	north
5.	rest	court	three	perish
6.	lark	grim	forests	brought

Provide English Spelling:

1.	[tɹi]	[gɾif]	[ˈkæɾʊl]	[ɑm]
2.	[θɾu]	[ˈflʊɾɪʃ]	[ɹʌn]	[mɔn]
3.	[ˈkwɔɾʊl]	[ɾɾum]	[dɹɔ]	[smɑt]

Answer Key:

1.	[fɹɛndz]	[θɾɛd]	[ˈʧɛɾɪʃt]	[gɑd]
2.	[ˈpæɾents]	[gɹin]	[sɔd]	[kɹɑs]
3.	[kɾʌʃt]	[wɔm]	[fɾut]	[ˈlɔɾʊlz]
4.	[tɾuθ]	[spɹɪŋ]	[ˈkɔɾʌs]	[nɔθ]
5.	[ɹɛst]	[kɔt]	[θɾi]	[ˈpɛɾɪʃ]
6.	[lɑk]	[gɾɪm]	[ˈfɔɾɛsts]	[bɹɔt]
1.	tree	grief	carol	arm
2.	through	flourish	run	morn
3.	quarrel	room	draw	smart

English Diphthongs

IPA	English	Transcription	Rules
[ɑːɪ]	sky	[skɑːɪ]	*i, ei, y* spellings
[ɛːɪ]	face	[fɛːɪs]	*a, ay, ey, ai, ei, ea* spellings
[ɔːɪ]	voice	[vɔːɪs]	*oi, oy* spellings
[aːʊ]	crown	[kɹaːʊn]	*ou, ow* spellings
[oːʊ]	soul	[soːʊl]	*o, ow, oa* spellings

The first vowel of a diphthong is long. Length is indicated by a long mark [ː].

Provide IPA:

1. way	child	boy	cry
2. brow	toil	rise	whole
3. spoil	those	town	break
4. down	shade	choice	thrives
5. twice	rose	they	boughs
6. road	found	old	coin

Provide English Spelling:

1. [snoːʊ]	[tɔːɪz]	[fɛːɪθ]	[ðaːʊ]
2. [ʍɑːɪl]	[saːʊθ]	[kɔːɪl]	[ʧɛːɪnʤ]
3. [ɛːɪʤ]	[kloːʊs]	[ɹaːʊnd]	[ʃɹɑːɪn]

Answer Key:

1. [wɛːɪ]	[ʧɑːɪld]	[bɔːɪ]	[kɹɑːɪ]
2. [bɹaːʊ]	[tɔːɪl]	[ɹɑːɪz]	[hoːʊl]
3. [spɔːɪl]	[ðoːʊz]	[taːʊn]	[bɹɛːɪk]
4. [daːʊn]	[ʃɛːɪd]	[ʧɔːɪs]	[θɹɑːɪvz]
5. [twɑːɪs]	[ɹoːʊz]	[ðɛːɪ]	[baːʊz]
6. [ɹoːʊd]	[faːʊnd]	[oːʊld]	[kɔːɪn]
1. snow	toys	faith	thou
2. while	south	coil	change
3. age	close	round	shrine

Vowel Replacement of "r"

The tongue position of a retroflex *r* has a negative effect on the tone. The final *r* of a word or element is replaced with [ʌ] in specified words.

English	IPA	English	IPA
dear	[dɪ:ʌ]	sure	[ʃʊ:ʌ]
care	[kɛ:ʌ]	fire	[fɑ:ɪʌ]
shore	[ʃɔ:ʌ]	sour	[sɑ:ʊʌ]

Provide IPA:

1. chores   there   fierce   spire

2. mire   cheer   cure   shares

3. tower   dire   square   wore

4. shores   flowers   wire   drear

5. air   squire   door   bower

6. sphere   dower   choirs   floors

Provide English Spelling:

1. [ʧɛ:ʌ]   [ʃɪ:ʌ]   [tɑ:ɪʌd]   [jɔ:ʌz]

2. [jɪ:ʌz]   [ˈdjʊ:ʌrɪŋ]   [kɑ:ʊʌz]   [ʍɛ:ʌ]

3. [ʃɑ:ʊʌ]   [skɛ:ʌs]   [ɹɔ:ʌd]   [ɪ:ʌz]

Answer Key:

1. [ʧɔ:ʌz]   [ðɛ:ʌ]   [fɪ:ʌs]   [spɑ:ɪʌ]
2. [mɑ:ɪʌ]   [ʧɪ:ʌ]   [kjʊ:ʌ]   [ʃɛ:ʌz]
3. [tɑ:ʊʌ]   [dɑ:ɪʌ]   [skwɛ:ʌ]   [wɔ:ʌ]
4. [ʃɔ:ʌz]   [flɑ:ʊʌz]   [wɑ:ɪʌ]   [dɹɪ:ʌ]
5. [ɛ:ʌ]   [skwɑ:ɪʌ]   [dɔ:ʌ]   [bɑ:ʊʌ]
6. [sfɪ:ʌ]   [dɑ:ʊʌ]   [kwɑ:ɪʌz]   [flɔ:ʌz]

1. chair   sheer   tired   yours
2. years   during   cowers   where
3. shower   scarce   roared   ears

Polysyllabic Words

IPA	English	Transcription	Rules
['] Stress mark	above	[ʌˈbʌv]	A stress mark is placed before the stressed syllable
[ə] Schwa	noble	[ˈnoːʊbəl] [ˈnoːʊbʊl]	The schwa represents vowels in unstressed syllables

The schwa stands for an undefined sound in an unstressed syllable. Defining schwa is based on spelling: *e* is [ɪ] or [ɛ]; *y* and *i* are [ɪ]; *a* is [æ] or [ʌ]; *o* and *u* are [ʌ]; vowel + *l* is [ʊ]; *a* or e + *r* is [ʌ]; *or* is [ɔ]; *ur* is [ʊ].

Provide IPA:

1. gracious   alone   horizon   linen

2. lifted   beauty   tender   sleeping

3. forbid   hidden   divine   welcome

4. happiness   crystal   leisure   moment

5. upon   palace   country   winter

6. maiden   remember   silent   because

Provide English Spelling:

1. [ʌˈnʌðʌ]   [ˈpɛːɪʃɛnt]   [ˈʤɛntʊl]   [dɪˈvaːɪdɛd]

2. [ˈvaːɪbɹænt]   [ˈmænʃʌn]   [fɔrˈɛvʌ]   [ˈgɹɛːɪtɛst]

3. [ˈwʌndɹʌs]   [dɪˈlaːɪt]   [ˈivnɪŋ]   [ˈɹɪvʌ]

Answer Key:

1. [ˈgɹɛːɪʃʌs]   [ʌˈloːʊn]   [hɔˈraːɪzʌn]   [ˈlɪnɛn]
2. [ˈlɪftɛd]   [ˈbjutɪ]   [ˈtɛndʌ]   [ˈslipɪŋ]
3. [fɔˈbɪd]   [ˈhɪdɛn]   [dɪˈvaːɪn]   [ˈwɛlkʌm]
4. [ˈhæpɪnɛs]   [ˈkɹɪstʊl]   [ˈliʒʊ]   [ˈmoːʊmɛnt]
5. [ʌˈpan]   [ˈpælæs]   [ˈkʌntɹɪ]   [ˈwɪntʌ]
6. [ˈmɛːɪdɛn]   [ɹɪˈmɛmbʌ]   [ˈsaːɪlɛnt]   [bɪˈkɔz]

1. another   patient   gentle   divided
2. vibrant   mansion   forever   greatest
3. wondrous   delight   evening   river

Review of English Transcription Rules

Provide IPA:

1.	adore	soothes	waltzed	rule
2.	true	usual	song	warrior
3.	showers	world	twilight	mixed
4.	charms	beware	wheels	crash
5.	books	drink	forgive	twins
6.	carry	swarm	thrills	awake
7.	endure	groan	August	tuned
8.	sought	appears	flew	begged
9.	vision	brown	desires	watched
10.	whose	flourish	gem	born
11.	wish	thaw	youth	rejoice

Answer Key:

1.	[ʌˈdɔːʌ]	[suðz]	[wɔltst]	[rrul]
2.	[tru]	[ˈjuʒuʊl]	[saŋ]	[ˈwɔjɔ]
3.	[ˈʃaːʊʌz]	[wɜld]	[ˈtwaːɪlaːɪt]	[mɪkst]
4.	[ʧamz]	[bɪˈwɛːʌ]	[ʍilz]	[kræʃ]
5.	[bʊks]	[dɹɪŋk]	[fɔˈgɪv]	[twɪnz]
6.	[ˈkæɾɪ]	[swɔm]	[θɾɪlz]	[ʌˈwɛːɪk]
7.	[ɪnˈdjʊːʌ]	[grоːʊn]	[ˈɔgʌst]	[tjund]
8.	[sɔt]	[ʌˈpɪːʌz]	[flu]	[bɛgd]
9.	[ˈvɪʒʌn]	[bɹɑːʊn]	[dɪˈzɑːɪʌz]	[waʧt]
10.	[huz]	[ˈflʊɾɪʃ]	[ʤɛm]	[bɔn]
11.	[wɪʃ]	[θɔ]	[juθ]	[ɪɪˈʤɔːɪs]

Phonetic Reading of English Text

The following lessons include daily phonetic assignments. General vocal principles are outlined in English on the even numbered pages with phonetic transcription of the text provided on the odd numbered pages. The daily assignment is to read the IPA and provide an English translation beneath the symbols. The exercise may be reversed by providing vowel symbols beneath the English words. This trains the singer to focus on the vowel line as represented by IPA. Test your skill by covering the left column and reading the IPA in the right column:

Art Song by Quilter, Roger (Eng. 1877 - 1953)

To Julia   [tu ˈdʒulɪʌ]
1. The bracelet   [ðʌ ˈbɹɛːɪslɛt]
Herrick, Robert (Eng. 1591 - 1674)

Why I tie about thy wrist,   [ʍaːɪ ɑːɪ taːɪ ʌˈbaːʊt ðɑːɪ ɹɪst]

Julia, this my silken twist;   [ˈdʒulɪʌ ðɪs maːɪ ˈsɪlkɛn twɪst]

For what other reason is 't,   [fɔ ʍat ˈʌðʌ ˈɹizʌn ɪzt]

But to show thee how, in part,   [bʌt tu ʃoːʊ ði haːʊ ɪn pat]

Thou my pretty captive art?   [ðaːʊ maːɪ ˈpɹɪtɪ ˈkæptɪv ɑt]

But thy bondslave is my heart;   [bʌt ðɑːɪ ˈbandslɛːɪv ɪz maːɪ hɑt]

'Tis but silk that bindeth thee,   [tɪz bʌt sɪlk ðæt ˈbaːɪndɛθ ði]

Knap the thread and thou art free: [næp ðʌ θrɛd ænd ðaːʊ ɑt fɹi]

But 'tis otherwise with me;   [bʌt tɪz ˈʌðʌwaːɪz wɪð mi]

I am bound, and fast bound, so   [ɑːɪ æm baːʊnd ænd fast baːʊnd soːʊ]

That from thee I cannot go;   [ðæt fɹʌm ði ɑːɪ kæˈnat goːʊ]

If I could, I would not so.   [ɪf ɑːɪ kʊd ɑːɪ wʊd nat soːʊ]

Correct vs Incorrect Postural Alignment

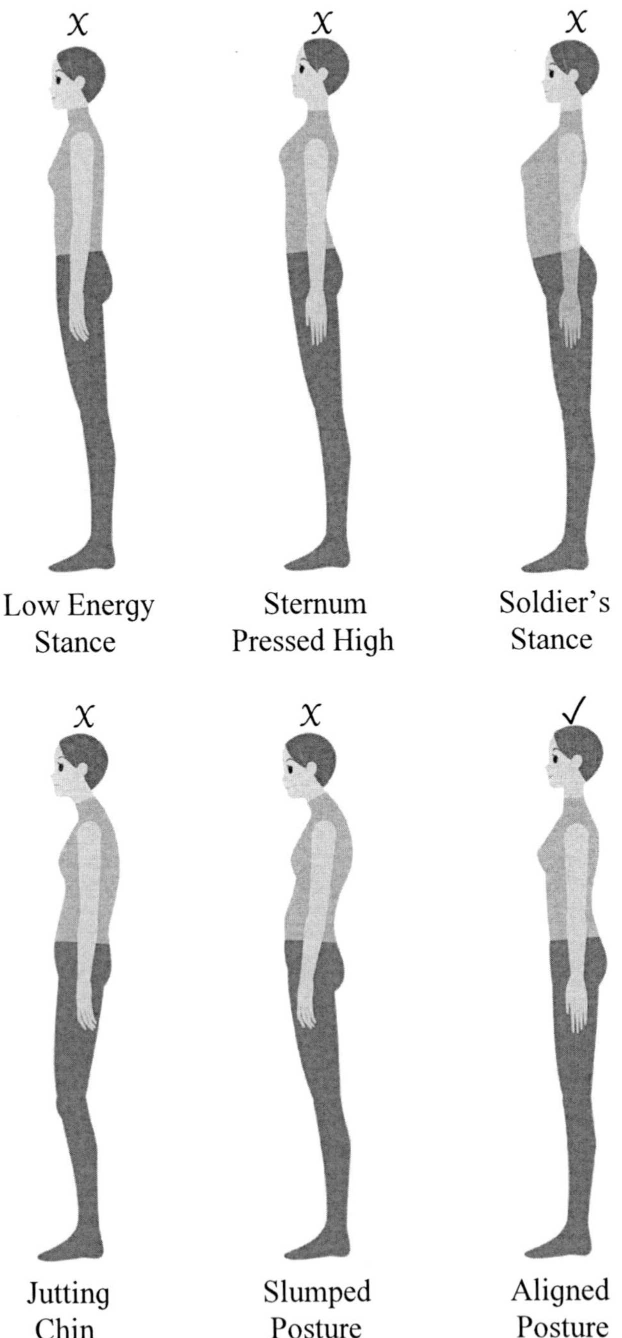

Postural Alignment: Week 3

Day 1: Exploring Upright, Expansive Posture

Day 2: Imagery

Day 3: Releasing Interfering Muscular Tension

Day 4: Diction Diagnostic

Day 5: Low Expansion for the Breath

Day 6: Efficient Use of the Air

Lesson Notes, Date: _____________

Checklist of Concepts to Review

BREATH
Breath Control___
p: 35, 63, 67
Breath Support___
p: 63, 65
Breath Expansion___
p: 33, 35
DICTION
Articulation___
p: 121, 123, 125, 131
Front Vowels___
p: 57, 105
Back Vowels___
p: 73, 107
Central Vowels___
p: 89, 91, 93, 109, 111
Mixed Vowels___
p: 113, 115
FLEXIBILITY
Flexibility___
p: 109, 139
MUSICIANSHIP
Artistry___
p: 141
Dynamics___
p: 143
Legato___
p: 49, 59, 75, 139, 141

POSTURE
Postural Alignment___
p: 25, 27
RANGE
Range___
p: 81, 91, 139
TONE
Chiaroscuro___
p: 97, 113, 115
Lip Trills___
p: 41, 43
Palatal Resonance___
p: 89, 91, 93, 109
Pharyngeal Space___
p: 57, 59, 93, 105, 109
Projection___
p: 73, 75, 93, 107
Register___
p: 43, 83
Resonance___
p: 93, 95, 97, 109, 137
Sensory Awareness___
p: 61, 127
Vibrato___
p: 43, 45, 51, 77, 79, 81
Vowel Equalization___
p: 79, 95, 137
WARM-UPS___
p: 200-204

WARNINGS
Breathy Tone___
p: 35, 77, 113, 125, 127
Faulty Formation___
p. 111, 127
Faulty Movement___
p. 45, 47
Faulty Onset___
p: 59, 75, 127
Jaw Tension___
p: 31, 111, 121, 123, 125
Nasal Tone ___
p: 111, 127
Pressed Tone___
p: 35, 41, 43, 83
Spread Tone___
p: 57, 61, 73, 111
Tension___
p: 29, 31, 45, 47, 61
Tongue Impeded Tone__
p: 111, 127
OTHER
Choral Singing___
p: 99
Stage Deportment___
p: 145
Vocal health___
p: 147

Daily Notes and Practice Times

Day 1   Practice Time:___________

Day 2   Practice Time:___________

Day 3   Practice Time:___________

Day 4   Practice Time:___________

Day 5   Practice Time:___________

Day 6   Practice Time:___________

Notes

Personal Assessment

Breath

Breath Control	70-------------79/80-------------89/90-------------100
Breath Expansion	70-------------79/80-------------89/90-------------100
Breath Support	70-------------79/80-------------89/90-------------100

Diction

Consonant Articulation	70-------------79/80-------------89/90-------------100
Vowel Formation	70-------------79/80-------------89/90-------------100

Musicianship

Expression	70-------------79/80-------------89/90-------------100
Legato	70-------------79/80-------------89/90-------------100
Pitch Accuracy	70-------------79/80-------------89/90-------------100
Rhythmic Accuracy	70-------------79/80-------------89/90-------------100

Posture and Tension

Postural Alignment	70-------------79/80-------------89/90-------------100
Release of Tension	70-------------79/80-------------89/90-------------100

Technique

Flexibility	70-------------79/80-------------89/90-------------100
Onset	70-------------79/80-------------89/90-------------100
Palatal Space	70-------------79/80-------------89/90-------------100
Pharyngeal Space	70-------------79/80-------------89/90-------------100
Projection	70-------------79/80-------------89/90-------------100
Vibrato	70-------------79/80-------------89/90-------------100
Tone Quality	70-------------79/80-------------89/90-------------100
Vowel Equalization	70-------------79/80-------------89/90-------------100

Exploring Upright, Expansive Posture

[ðɛːɐɾ ɑ ˈsɛvɛn ˈætɹɪbjuts ʌv gʊd ˈpastʃʊ (si ˈɪmædʒ an pɛːɪdʒ ˈtwɛntɪ)]:

1. [ðʌ spɑːɪn ɪz ɪˈlaŋgɛːɪtɛd]

2. [ðʌ skʌl ɪz ˈbælænst an ðʌ spɑːɪn]

3. [ðʌ fit fil ˈɹɹutɛd]

4. [ðʌ ˈbadɪ ɪz ˈbælænst ænd ʌˈlɑːɪnd]

5. [ðʌ ɹɪb kɛːɪdʒ filz ˈoːʊpɛn ænd ɪkˈspændɛd]

6. [ðʌ stans ɪz ˈbɔːɹænt ænd ɹˈlæstɪk]

7. [ðʌ ˈpastʃʊ mɛːɪnˈtɛːɪnz ʌ ˈnoːʊbʊl stans]

The Rag Doll Stretch Exercise ~ Clifton Ware

[ˈmʌltɪpʊl ˈkansɛpts aɾ ɪnˈkɔpɔɹɛːɪtɛd ɪn wʌn ˈsɪmpʊl ʌˈsɑːɪnmɛnt]:

1. [bɛnd æt ðʌ wɛːɪst ænd swɪŋ ði amz]

2. [ˈnoːʊtɪs ðʌ ˈfɔlʌwɛːɪˈfilɪŋ ɪn ðʌ ˈʃoːʊldʌz]

3. [stɹɛtʃ ði amz ˈʌpwʊd twɔd ðʌ ˈsilɪŋ]

4. [mɛːɪnˈtɛːɪn ðʌ poˈzɪʃʌn ʌv ðʌ ˈstɜnʌm]

5. [plɛːɪs ʌ ˈfɪŋgʌɾ an ðʌ ˈstɜnʌm ðɛn ɹɪˈlis ænd ˈloːʊʌ ði amz]

6. [ˈɹɛplɪkɛːɪt ðʌ ˈfɔlʌwɛːɪˈfilɪŋ ɪn ðʌ ˈʃoːʊldʌz nɛk ænd dʒɔ]

Notes

Personal Assessment

Breath
Breath Control   70-------------79/80-------------89/90-------------100
Breath Expansion   70-------------79/80-------------89/90-------------100
Breath Support   70-------------79/80-------------89/90-------------100

Diction
Consonant Articulation 70-------------79/80-------------89/90-------------100
Vowel Formation   70-------------79/80-------------89/90-------------100

Musicianship
Expression   70-------------79/80-------------89/90-------------100
Legato   70-------------79/80-------------89/90-------------100
Pitch Accuracy   70-------------79/80-------------89/90-------------100
Rhythmic Accuracy   70-------------79/80-------------89/90-------------100

Posture and Tension
Postural Alignment   70-------------79/80-------------89/90-------------100
Release of Tension   70-------------79/80-------------89/90-------------100

Technique
Flexibility   70-------------79/80-------------89/90-------------100
Onset   70-------------79/80-------------89/90-------------100
Palatal Space   70-------------79/80-------------89/90-------------100
Pharyngeal Space   70-------------79/80-------------89/90-------------100
Projection   70-------------79/80-------------89/90-------------100
Vibrato   70-------------79/80-------------89/90-------------100
Tone Quality   70-------------79/80-------------89/90-------------100
Vowel Equalization   70-------------79/80-------------89/90-------------100

The Tree Image

[ðɪs ˈɛksʌsaːɪz fɹʌm ʌ bæˈlɛːɪ klas kʌmˈpɛːʌz ˈpasʧʊ wɪð tɹi ɡɹoːʊθ]:

1. [tɛːɪk af jɔːʌ ʃuz soːʊ ðæt jɔːʌ fit kæn fil ðʌ flɔːʌ]

2. [ðʌ fit ɑ ˈslaːɪtlɪ ʌˈpat wɪð ðʌ ˈdamɪnænt fʊt ˈfɔwʊd]

3. [ɪˈmædʒɪn jɔːʌ toːʊz a rɹuts ɡɹoːʊɪŋ ˈɪntu ðʌ ɡɹaːʊnd]

4. [ðʌ ˈstɜnʌm ænd hɛd ɑ ˈbɹanʧɛz ɡɹoːʊɪŋ twɔd ðʌ sʌn]

5. [ɹɪˈlis jɔːʌ hɛd fɹʌm ðʌ spaːɪn æz ɪf ɪt wɜr ʌ tap bɹanʧ]

6. [ðʌ kɹaːʊn ʌv jɔːʌ hɛd (ˈpoːʊnɪtɛːɪl) ɪz ðʌ ˈtɔlɛst lɪm]

The Diver Image ~ William McIver

[ˈmɪmɪk ðʌ ˈbɔːɹænt stans ʌv ʌ ˈdaːɪvʌr æt ði ɛdʒ ʌv ʌ ˈdaːɪvɪŋ bɔd]

[faːɪnd ʌ ˈbælænst ænd ˈɛnʌdʒaːɪzd poːʊz ðæt ɪz ˈɹɛdɪ fɔr ækˈtɪvɪtɪ]

Warnings

[ʌˈvɔːɪd ʌ stɪf stans ænd du nat stænd wɪð ðʌ fit kloːʊs tuˈɡɛðʌ]

[ʌ slʌmpt ˈpasʧʊr ɪz nat pɹɪˈpɛːʌd fɔ ðʌ dɪˈmandz ʌv ˈsɪŋɪŋ]

[ðʌ ʧin ʃʊd nat dʒʌt ˈfɔwʊd nɔ bi tʌkt ɪn]

[du nat ɹɛːɪz ðʌ ˈʃoːʊldʌz nɔ pɹɛs ðʌ ʧɛst haːɪ]

[si ɪɡˈzampʊlz ʌv ɪnkɔˈɹɛkt pasʧʊr an pɛːɪdʒ ˈtwɛntɪ]

Notes

Personal Assessment

Breath
Breath Control   70-------------79/80-------------89/90-------------100
Breath Expansion   70-------------79/80-------------89/90-------------100
Breath Support   70-------------79/80-------------89/90-------------100

Diction
Consonant Articulation   70-------------79/80-------------89/90-------------100
Vowel Formation   70-------------79/80-------------89/90-------------100

Musicianship
Expression   70-------------79/80-------------89/90-------------100
Legato   70-------------79/80-------------89/90-------------100
Pitch Accuracy   70-------------79/80-------------89/90-------------100
Rhythmic Accuracy   70-------------79/80-------------89/90-------------100

Posture and Tension
Postural Alignment   70-------------79/80-------------89/90-------------100
Release of Tension   70-------------79/80-------------89/90-------------100

Technique
Flexibility   70-------------79/80-------------89/90-------------100
Onset   70-------------79/80-------------89/90-------------100
Palatal Space   70-------------79/80-------------89/90-------------100
Pharyngeal Space   70-------------79/80-------------89/90-------------100
Projection   70-------------79/80-------------89/90-------------100
Vibrato   70-------------79/80-------------89/90-------------100
Tone Quality   70-------------79/80-------------89/90-------------100
Vowel Equalization   70-------------79/80-------------89/90-------------100

Releasing Interfering Muscular Tension

[ðɛːʌɾ ɑ ɛːɪt 'ɛːʌɾɪʌz ʌv ðʌ 'badɪ pɹoːʊn tu ʌ'nɛsɪsɛɾɪ 'tɛnʃʌn]:

1. [ʤɔ]   5. [lɪps]

2. [nɛk]   6. [ʧiks]

3. [tʌŋ]   7. [ɑːɪ bɹɑːʊz]

4. ['ʃoːʊldʌz]   8. ['ʌndʌamz]

['tɛnʃʌn ɹɪ'zʌlts ɪn 'mʌsʊl ɹɪ'ʤɪdɪtɪ ðæt kæn bi fɛlt ænd sin]

['sɪŋʌz mʌst ɑːɪ'dɛntɪfɑːɪ ænd ɹɪ'lis ˌɪntʌ'fɪːʌɾɪŋ 'mʌskjulʌ 'tɛnʃʌn]

['tɛnʃʌn ɪz ɹɪ'list θɾu 'muvmɛnt tʌʧ ɔ dɪs'tɹækʃʌn]:

1. [ʌ 'mʌsʊl ɪn 'moːʊʃʌn kæ'nat kɹæmp tu ðʌ pɔːɪnt ʌv 'biɪŋ 'ɹɪʤɪd]

2. [tʌʧ ɪntʌ'ɾʌpts ðʌ nɜv 'ɪmpʌlsɛz ðæt ɹɪ'zʌlt ɪn 'nɛgʌtɪv 'tɛnʃʌn]

3. [ɹɪ'plɛːɪs 'nɛgʌtɪv 'mʌsʊl æk'tɪvɪtɪ wɪð æn ʌ'poːʊzɪŋ 'muvmɛnt]

Muscle Awareness Exercise

['pɹæktɪs ðʌ ɹæg dal stɹɛʧ 'ɛksʌsɑːɪz ɪn fɹʌnt ʌv ʌ 'mɪɾɔ (pɛːɪʤ 25)]

['ɹɛplɪkɛːɪt ðʌ 'fɔlʌwɛːɪ'filɪŋ ɪn ði ɛːɪt 'ɛːʌɾɪʌz 'lɪstɛd ʌ'bʌv]

[ði ɛːɪt 'ɛːʌɾɪʌz ɑɾ ʌ'pɛndæʤɛz ðæt hæŋ af æn ʌ'lɑːɪnd 'sɛntɹʊl kɔːʌ]

[ɪn'hans ðʌ fil ʌv ɹɪ'lis bɑːɪ ɾɪ'pitɪŋ ðʌ 'faloːʊɪŋ 'kwɛːɪkʌ fɹɛːɪz]:

[pis æt ðʌ 'sɛntʌ]

Notes

Personal Assessment

Breath
Breath Control   70-------------79/80-------------89/90-------------100
Breath Expansion   70-------------79/80-------------89/90-------------100
Breath Support   70-------------79/80-------------89/90-------------100

Diction
Consonant Articulation 70-------------79/80-------------89/90-------------100
Vowel Formation   70-------------79/80-------------89/90-------------100

Musicianship
Expression   70-------------79/80-------------89/90-------------100
Legato   70-------------79/80-------------89/90-------------100
Pitch Accuracy   70-------------79/80-------------89/90-------------100
Rhythmic Accuracy   70-------------79/80-------------89/90-------------100

Posture and Tension
Postural Alignment   70-------------79/80-------------89/90-------------100
Release of Tension   70-------------79/80-------------89/90-------------100

Technique
Flexibility   70-------------79/80-------------89/90-------------100
Onset   70-------------79/80-------------89/90-------------100
Palatal Space   70-------------79/80-------------89/90-------------100
Pharyngeal Space   70-------------79/80-------------89/90-------------100
Projection   70-------------79/80-------------89/90-------------100
Vibrato   70-------------79/80-------------89/90-------------100
Tone Quality   70-------------79/80-------------89/90-------------100
Vowel Equalization   70-------------79/80-------------89/90-------------100

Diction Diagnostic

[ʌbˈzɜv ðʌ ˈkantækt bɪˈtwin ði aˈtɪkjulɛːɪtɔz tu ˈmanɪtʌ ˈtɛnʃʌn]:

    1. [fɔm [b] wɪð ˈtɑːɪtlɪ pɹɛst lɪps]

    2. [tʌʧ ðʌ sɑːɪdz ʌv ðʌ θroːʊt bɪˈniθ ðʌ ʧɪn]

    3. [fil hɑːʊ ðʌ nɛk ˈmʌsʊlz ˈtɑːɪtɛn ɪn ɹɪˈspɑns]

    4. [sʌˈstɛːɪn ʌ [m] wɪð ðʌ lɪps ˈbɛːʌlɪ ˈtʌʧɪŋ]

    5. [ðʌ lɪps ˈtɪŋgʊl ʍɛn lɑːɪt ˈkantækt ɪz ʌˈʧivd (si pɛːɪʤ 36)]

[lɑːɪt ˈkantækt ˈɛnʌʤɑːɪzɛz ðʌ ˈdɪkʃʌn ænd ɪnˈhansɛz flɛksɪˈbɪlɪtɪ]

There is "tension" required for singing, but that tension should be as low in the body and as far away from the area of the throat, jaw, and tongue as possible. Lindsey Christiansen

[ˈtɛnʃʌn æt ðʌ tʌŋ bɛːɪs ɪz ɹɪˈlist wɪð tʌŋ aʧ ˈɛksʌsɑːɪzɛz]:

Maintain the space of [a] through-out the exercise. See page 92 for a description of central [a].

[ˈɔltʌnɛːɪt bɪˈtwin bɑːɪˈlɛːɪbɪʊlz ænd ˈdɛntʊlz tu ɹɪˈlis ðʌ lɪp ænd tʌŋ]:

[la   be da   me ni   po tu   la   be] ~ *Barbara Honn*

Let the articulators articulate and not support. One of the major problems for both diction and fine singing is that the articulators often try to be the supporters. Lindsey Christiansen

Notes

Personal Assessment

Breath
Breath Control   70-------------79/80-------------89/90-------------100
Breath Expansion   70-------------79/80-------------89/90-------------100
Breath Support   70-------------79/80-------------89/90-------------100

Diction
Consonant Articulation   70-------------79/80-------------89/90-------------100
Vowel Formation   70-------------79/80-------------89/90-------------100

Musicianship
Expression   70-------------79/80-------------89/90-------------100
Legato   70-------------79/80-------------89/90-------------100
Pitch Accuracy   70-------------79/80-------------89/90-------------100
Rhythmic Accuracy   70-------------79/80-------------89/90-------------100

Posture and Tension
Postural Alignment   70-------------79/80-------------89/90-------------100
Release of Tension   70-------------79/80-------------89/90-------------100

Technique
Flexibility   70-------------79/80-------------89/90-------------100
Onset   70-------------79/80-------------89/90-------------100
Palatal Space   70-------------79/80-------------89/90-------------100
Pharyngeal Space   70-------------79/80-------------89/90-------------100
Projection   70-------------79/80-------------89/90-------------100
Vibrato   70-------------79/80-------------89/90-------------100
Tone Quality   70-------------79/80-------------89/90-------------100
Vowel Equalization   70-------------79/80-------------89/90-------------100

Low Expansion for the Breath

[ðʌ bɹɛθ ɪkˈspænʃʌn fɔ ˈsɪŋɪŋ ɪz ˈloːʊʌ ðæn ðæt ʌv spiʧ]

[ðʌ ˈsɪŋʌz ɪkˈspænʃʌn ʌˈkɜz bɪˈloːʊ ðʌ wɛːɪst ænd ʌˈɹaːʊnd ðʌ ˈbɑdɪ]

[ɪt meːɪ fil ˈɔkwʊd bʌt nat ˈstɹɛnjuʌs tu ɪkˈspænd ðʌ ˈloːʊʌ ˈæbdomɛn]

Experiencing a Low Expansion for the Breath

1. [sɪt wɪð ˈɛlboːʊz an ðʌ niz ænd ʧɪn ɪn ðʌ pɑmz]

2. [ɪnˈhɛːɪl ænd fil ɪkˈspænʃʌn ɪn ðʌ ˈloːʊʌ bæk ˈɹidʒʌn]

3. [lɛːɪ wɪð jɔːʌ ˈʌpʌ bæk ænd ˈʃoːʊldʌz flæt an ðʌ floːʌ]

4. [plɛːɪs ʌ bʊk an jɔːʌ ˈstʌmæk bɪˈloːʊ ðʌ ˈbɛlɪ ˈbʌtʌn]

5. [ɪnˈhɛːɪl ænd ʌbˈzɜv ði ɪkˈspænʃʌn ɪn ðʌ ˈloːʊʌ ˈæbdomɛn]

6. [stænd ænd ˈɹɛplɪkɛːɪt ðʌ ˈpasʧʊr ʌv ˈnʌmbʌ θɹi ʌˈbʌv]

7. [ɪnˈhɛːɪl ʌ [w] an ˈsɛvɛn kaːʊnts wɪð ɪkˈspænʃʌn bɪˈloːʊ ðʌ wɛːɪst]

8. [fɔɹɪ ʌ [s] wɪðˈaːʊt ˈpɹɛsɪŋ ði aˈtɪkjulɛːɪtɔz]

9. [ɪkˈspɛl ɔl ði ɛːʌɾ aˈtɪkjulɛːɪtɪŋ ðʌ [s] an ˈsɛvɛn kaːʊnts]

10. [mɛːɪnˈtɛːɪn ʌ kʌnˈsɪstɛnt floːʊ ʌv ˈæspɪɾɛːɪtɛd saːʊnd]

Additional Goals

[ɪnˈhɛːɪl ʌ ˈsjutʌbʊl ʌˈmaːʊnt ʌv ɛːʌ tu mit ðʌ dɪˈmandz ʌv ðʌ fɹɛːɪz]

[ˈðʌ ˈdaːɪʌfɹæm muvz ʍaːɪl ðʌ ɹɪbz ænd ˈstɜnʌm stɛːɪ kam ænd ɹɪˈlɪst]

Notes

Personal Assessment

Breath
Breath Control   70-------------79/80-------------89/90-------------100
Breath Expansion   70-------------79/80-------------89/90-------------100
Breath Support   70-------------79/80-------------89/90-------------100

Diction
Consonant Articulation 70-------------79/80-------------89/90-------------100
Vowel Formation   70-------------79/80-------------89/90-------------100

Musicianship
Expression   70-------------79/80-------------89/90-------------100
Legato   70-------------79/80-------------89/90-------------100
Pitch Accuracy   70-------------79/80-------------89/90-------------100
Rhythmic Accuracy   70-------------79/80-------------89/90-------------100

Posture and Tension
Postural Alignment   70-------------79/80-------------89/90-------------100
Release of Tension   70-------------79/80-------------89/90-------------100

Technique
Flexibility   70-------------79/80-------------89/90-------------100
Onset   70-------------79/80-------------89/90-------------100
Palatal Space   70-------------79/80-------------89/90-------------100
Pharyngeal Space   70-------------79/80-------------89/90-------------100
Projection   70-------------79/80-------------89/90-------------100
Vibrato   70-------------79/80-------------89/90-------------100
Tone Quality   70-------------79/80-------------89/90-------------100
Vowel Equalization   70-------------79/80-------------89/90-------------100

Efficient Use of the Air

The breath for singing should be a response to the musical phrase one is about to sing – the thought of the phrase should inspire the breath.
Cynthia Hoffmann

[ɪˈfɪʃent jus ʌv ði ɛːʌɾ ɪz ʤʌst æz ɪmˈpɔtænt æz ði ɪnhʌˈlɛːɪʃʌn]

[bɹɪð ɪn ðʌ ʃɛːɪp ʌv ðʌ ˈvɑːʊʌl]

[du nat hoːʊld ði ɛːʌɾ ɪn ˈnɑːɪðʌ fɔs ɪt ɑːʊt]

[ʌˈlɑːʊ ðʌ bɹɛθ tu floːʊ ɑːʊt ɪn ʌ fɑːɪn stɹim ʌv ɛːʌ]

[ɪˈmæʤɪn ɹɪˈlisɪŋ ðʌ bɹɛθ θɾu ʌ stɹɔ]

[ʌ ˈkændʊl waz juzd ɪn ðʌ bɛl ˈkanto ˈpɹːʌɾɪʌd tu ˈmanɪtʌ ɛːʌ floːʊ]

[ðʌ ˈsɪŋʌ waz askt tu sɪŋ nɪːʌ ðʌ flɛːɪm]

[ðʌ toːʊn waz kʌnˈsɪdʌd pɹɛst ɪf ðʌ flɛːɪm ˈflɪkʌd]

Warnings

Note: [ʌ plænd ɪnhʌˈlɛːɪʃʌn ʌˈlɑːʊz ðʌ ˈsɪŋʌ tu ɾɪˈlis ɔl ði ɛːʌ]

[du nat ˈɹɛːɪz ðʌ ˈstɜnʌm ɔ ˈʃoːʊldʌz ʌˈpan ɪnhʌˈlɛːɪʃʌn]

[ʌ lɑːʊd bɹɛθ ˈɪndɪkɛːɪts ɹɪˈstɹɪkʃʌn wɪðˈɪn ði ɛːʌ ˈpæsæʤ]

[ˈpækɪŋ ʌp æn ɪkˈsɛsɪv ʌˈmɑːʊnt ʌv ɛːʌ ˈkɔzɛz ˈtɛnʃʌn]

[du nat ʌˈlɑːʊ ðʌ ɹɪbz tu koˈlæps]

[slʌmpt ˈpasʧʊ dʌz nat ʌˈkamodɛːɪt ʌ loːʊ ɪkˈspænʃʌn fɔ ðʌ bɹɛθ]

Formation Indicates Tension in the Voice
(see page 31)

Incorrect Formation of Bilabial Consonants

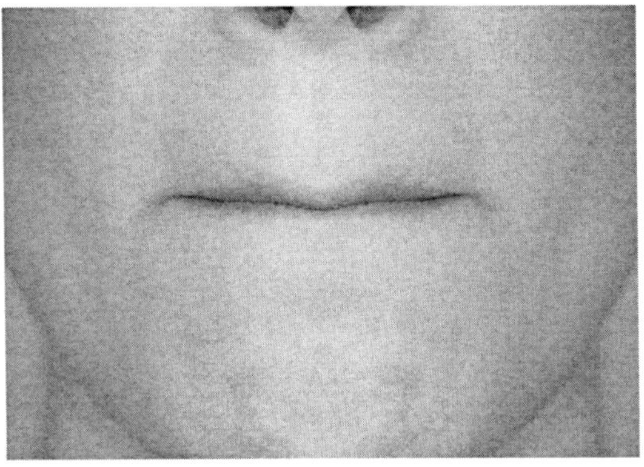

The tone is constricted when the lips are curled in for *m, b,* and *p*. Pressed contact between the articulators initiates negative tension and muffles the consonant sound.

Correct Formation of Bilabial Consonants

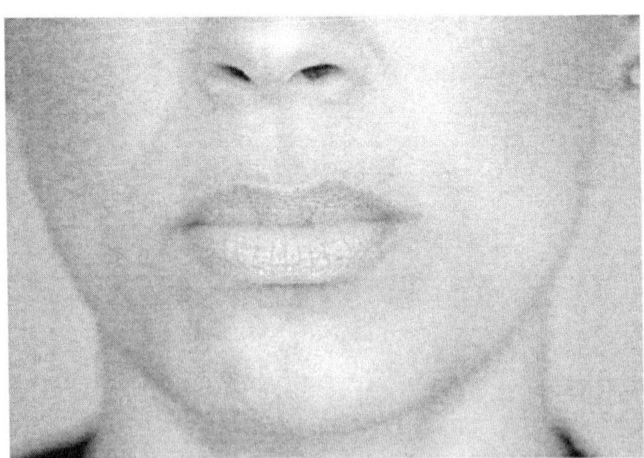

The tone is free to vibrate when the lips barely touch for consonants *m, b,* and *p*.

Lip Trills and [ŋ]: Week 4

Day 1: Exploring Vibrato – Lip Trills

Day 2: Lip and Tongue Trill Exercises

Day 3: Identifying Interfering Muscular
Movement

Day 4: Remedies

Day 5: Exploring Legato

Day 6: Incorporating Vibrato

Lesson Notes, Date: _____________

Checklist of Concepts to Review

BREATH
Breath Control___
p: 35, 63, 67
Breath Support___
p: 63, 65
Breath Expansion___
p: 33, 35
DICTION
Articulation___
p: 121, 123, 125, 131
Front Vowels___
p: 57, 105
Back Vowels___
p: 73, 107
Central Vowels___
p: 89, 91, 93, 109, 111
Mixed Vowels___
p: 113, 115
FLEXIBILITY
Flexibility___
p: 109, 139
MUSICIANSHIP
Artistry___
p: 141
Dynamics___
p: 143
Legato___
p: 49, 59, 75, 139, 141

POSTURE
Postural Alignment___
p: 25, 27
RANGE
Range___
p: 81, 91, 139
TONE
Chiaroscuro___
p: 97, 113, 115
Lip Trills___
p: 41, 43
Palatal Resonance___
p: 89, 91, 93, 109
Pharyngeal Space___
p: 57, 59, 93, 105, 109
Projection___
p: 73, 75, 93, 107
Register___
p: 43, 83
Resonance___
p: 93, 95, 97, 109, 137
Sensory Awareness___
p: 61, 127
Vibrato___
p: 43, 45, 51, 77, 79, 81
Vowel Equalization___
p: 79, 95, 137
WARM-UPS___
p: 200-204

WARNINGS
Breathy Tone___
p: 35, 77, 113, 125, 127
Faulty Formation___
p. 111, 127
Faulty Movement___
p. 45, 47
Faulty Onset___
p: 59, 75, 127
Jaw Tension___
p: 31, 111, 121, 123, 125
Nasal Tone ___
p: 111, 127
Pressed Tone___
p: 35, 41, 43, 83
Spread Tone___
p: 57, 61, 73, 111
Tension___
p: 29, 31, 45, 47, 61
Tongue Impeded Tone___
p: 111, 127
OTHER
Choral Singing___
p: 99
Stage Deportment___
p: 145
Vocal health___
p: 147

Daily Notes and Practice Times

Day 1   Practice Time:__________

Day 2   Practice Time:__________

Day 3   Practice Time:__________

Day 4   Practice Time:__________

Day 5   Practice Time:__________

Day 6   Practice Time:__________

Notes

Personal Assessment

Breath
Breath Control   70--------------79/80--------------89/90--------------100
Breath Expansion   70--------------79/80--------------89/90--------------100
Breath Support   70--------------79/80--------------89/90--------------100

Diction
Consonant Articulation 70--------------79/80--------------89/90--------------100
Vowel Formation   70--------------79/80--------------89/90--------------100

Musicianship
Expression   70--------------79/80--------------89/90--------------100
Legato   70--------------79/80--------------89/90--------------100
Pitch Accuracy   70--------------79/80--------------89/90--------------100
Rhythmic Accuracy   70--------------79/80--------------89/90--------------100

Posture and Tension
Postural Alignment   70--------------79/80--------------89/90--------------100
Release of Tension   70--------------79/80--------------89/90--------------100

Technique
Flexibility   70--------------79/80--------------89/90--------------100
Onset   70--------------79/80--------------89/90--------------100
Palatal Space   70--------------79/80--------------89/90--------------100
Pharyngeal Space   70--------------79/80--------------89/90--------------100
Projection   70--------------79/80--------------89/90--------------100
Vibrato   70--------------79/80--------------89/90--------------100
Tone Quality   70--------------79/80--------------89/90--------------100
Vowel Equalization   70--------------79/80--------------89/90--------------100

Exploring Vibrato – Lip Trills

[ʌ ˈmastʌɾɪ ʌv ˈmʌltɪpʊl skɪlz ɪz ˈnidɛd ɪn ˈɔdʌ tu dɪsˈkʌvʌ vɑːɪˈbɹatoːʊ]

[lɪp tɹɪlz ɹɪˈkwaːɪʌɾ ʌ ˈmɪnɪmʊl ʌˈmaːʊnt ʌv ˈmʌskjulʌɾ ɪnˈvalvmɛnt]

[ðɛːɪ mɛːɪk ðʌ ˈsɪŋʌ fil æz ɪf ðʌ θɾoːʊt ɪz ˈbaːɪpast ɔl tuˈgɛðʌ]

[lɪp tɹɪlz gɪv ðʌ ˈsɪŋʌ ðʌ ˈfɹidʌm tu ˈfoːʊkʌs an]:

    1. [pastʃʊ]   4. [ˈɹɛzonæns]

    2. [bɹɛθ]   5. [vɑːɪˈbɹatoːʊ]

    3. [ɹɪˈlis ʌv ˌɪntʌˈfɪːɾɪŋ ˈmʌskjulʌ ˈtɛnʃʌn]

Vibrato is breath moving past a released apparatus whether it be the lips (lip trill), the tongue (rolled r), or the larynx (vibrato).

[ˈfʊlɪ vɔːɪs ʌ saft lɪp tɹɪl ænd bi ʌˈwɛːɾ ʌv ɪts ˈɹɛzoˌnɛːɪtɪŋ ˈɔɾɪdʒɪn]

[ʌ lɪp tɹɪl mɛːɪ fil ɔ saːʊnd æz ɪf ɪt ˈɛmænɛːɪts fɹʌm]:

    1. [ðʌ saːʊnd ʌv ˈflæpɪŋ lɪps]

    2. [ðʌ θɾoːʊt ɔ [h] ˈkansonænt]

    3. [æn ˈɛːɾɪʌ ɪn ðʌ haːɪt ʌv ðʌ jon spɛːɪs]

[ðʌ lɪps ʃʊd fil æz ɪf ðɛːɪ a ðʌ sɔs ʌv ðʌ saːʊnd]

[ðʌ saːʊnd ʌv ˈbɹɛθɪnɛs ˈɪndɪkɛːɪts ʌ ˈhɛvɪ ɔ pɹɛst ɛːʌ floːʊ]

[ɪkˈsplɔːʌ fʌˈɾɪndʒʊl ˈspɛːɪs baːɪ ˈfɔmɪŋ [i] ʍaːɪl ˈtɹɪlɪŋ]

Notes

Personal Assessment

Breath
Breath Control   70-------------79/80-------------89/90-------------100
Breath Expansion   70-------------79/80-------------89/90-------------100
Breath Support   70-------------79/80-------------89/90-------------100

Diction
Consonant Articulation 70-------------79/80-------------89/90-------------100
Vowel Formation   70-------------79/80-------------89/90-------------100

Musicianship
Expression   70-------------79/80-------------89/90-------------100
Legato   70-------------79/80-------------89/90-------------100
Pitch Accuracy   70-------------79/80-------------89/90-------------100
Rhythmic Accuracy   70-------------79/80-------------89/90-------------100

Posture and Tension
Postural Alignment   70-------------79/80-------------89/90-------------100
Release of Tension   70-------------79/80-------------89/90-------------100

Technique
Flexibility   70-------------79/80-------------89/90-------------100
Onset   70-------------79/80-------------89/90-------------100
Palatal Space   70-------------79/80-------------89/90-------------100
Pharyngeal Space   70-------------79/80-------------89/90-------------100
Projection   70-------------79/80-------------89/90-------------100
Vibrato   70-------------79/80-------------89/90-------------100
Tone Quality   70-------------79/80-------------89/90-------------100
Vowel Equalization   70-------------79/80-------------89/90-------------100

Lip and Tongue Trills

[mɔːʌ ðæn wʌn pɪʧ ɪz ˈnidɛd ɪn ˈɔdʌ tu kɹɪˈɛːɪt ʌ ˈvaːɪbɹænt toːʊn]

[ðʌ pɪʧ muvz ɪn wʌn ʌv θɾi wɛːɪz]:

    1. [ɑn ænd ʌˈɾaːʊnd ðʌ ˈpɹɑːɪmɛɾɪ noːʊt]

    2. [ɑn ænd bɪˈloːʊ ðʌ ˈpɹɑːɪmɛɾɪ noːʊt]

    3. [ɑn ænd ʌˈbʌv ðʌ ˈpɹɑːɪmɛɾɪ noːʊt]

Note: vibrato that pulsates on the same pitch produces a goat's bleat.

[ʌ lɪp tɹɪl ðæt ɪz ˈsɛntʌd ɑn ænd ʌˈbʌv ðʌ ˈpɹɑːɪmɛɾɪ noːʊt ɪz ˈɑptɪmʊl]

[ˈvaːɪbɹænsɪ ʌˈkɜz ʍɛn ðʌ ˈkansɛpt ʌv ɹɪˈlisɪŋ ðʌ pɪʧ ɪz dɪsˈkʌvʌd]

[ɪkˈsplɔːʌ ˈsɛmaːɪtoːʊnz baːɪ ˈslaːɪdɪŋ ɑn ðʌ ʃap saːɪd ʌv ðʌ toːʊn]

[ˈʃapɪŋ ˈmɜʤɛz dɪˈsɛndɪŋ toːʊnz ænd dʌz nat ʌˈkamodɛːɪt ˈbɛltɪŋ]

Lip trill: 5 slide 1   Lip trill: 5   4   3   2   1

[sɪŋ ði ˈɛksʌsaːɪz ʌˈbʌv wɪð ʌ ˈfʊlɪ vɔːɪst ɹoːʊld "r"]

[lɪp tɹɪl ðʌ ˈfaloːʊɪŋ ˈsikwɛns ʃapɪŋ ðʌ faːɪv ænd ɛːɪt]:

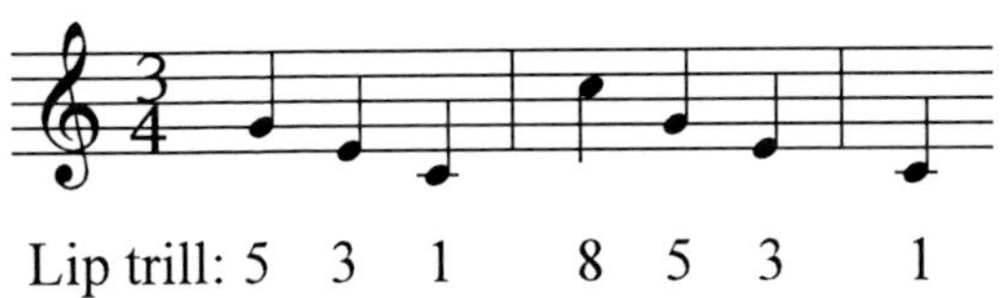

Lip trill: 5   3   1   8   5   3   1

Notes

Personal Assessment

Breath

Breath Control	70--------------79/80--------------89/90--------------100		
Breath Expansion	70--------------79/80--------------89/90--------------100		
Breath Support	70--------------79/80--------------89/90--------------100		

Diction

Consonant Articulation 70--------------79/80--------------89/90--------------100
Vowel Formation 70--------------79/80--------------89/90--------------100

Musicianship

Expression 70--------------79/80--------------89/90--------------100
Legato 70--------------79/80--------------89/90--------------100
Pitch Accuracy 70--------------79/80--------------89/90--------------100
Rhythmic Accuracy 70--------------79/80--------------89/90--------------100

Posture and Tension

Postural Alignment 70--------------79/80--------------89/90--------------100
Release of Tension 70--------------79/80--------------89/90--------------100

Technique

Flexibility 70--------------79/80--------------89/90--------------100
Onset 70--------------79/80--------------89/90--------------100
Palatal Space 70--------------79/80--------------89/90--------------100
Pharyngeal Space 70--------------79/80--------------89/90--------------100
Projection 70--------------79/80--------------89/90--------------100
Vibrato 70--------------79/80--------------89/90--------------100
Tone Quality 70--------------79/80--------------89/90--------------100
Vowel Equalization 70--------------79/80--------------89/90--------------100

Identifying Interfering Muscular Movement

[ˈmʌskjulʌɾ ɪnˈtæŋgʊlmɛnts ˈæktɪvɛːɪt ˈfɪzɪkʊl ɹɪˈspansɛz]

[ɪntʌˈfɪːʌɾɪŋ ˈmʌskjulʌ ˈtɛnʃʌn mɛːɪ kɔz ðʌ ˈsɪŋʌ tu]:

1. [mak pɪʧ ˈʧɛːɪndʒɛz wɪð ðʌ ˈbadɪ (ɹɛːɪz ðʌ ʧɪn fɔɾ ʌˈsɛndɪŋ noːʊts)]

2. [mak ðʌ ˈtɛmpoːʊ wɪð ðʌ ˈbadɪ (nad ðʌ hɛd tu ðʌ bit)]

3. [twɪʧ æn ˈɛːʌɾɪʌ ʌv ðʌ ˈbadɪ (ʃɛːɪk ðʌ hænd tu ɪnˈhans vaːɪˈbɹatoːʊ)]

4. [fɔm ˈvaːʊʌlz ɪnkɔˈɾɛktlɪ (smaːɪl tu ik aːʊt ʌ haːɪ noːʊt)]

Remedy for Marking Pitch Changes

[ˈtɹænsfʌ ˈtɛnʃʌn ðæt faːɪndz ʌ ˈfɔltɪ ˈaːʊt ˌlɛt ˈɪntu bɹɛθ ˈɛnʌdʒɪ]

[dɪsˈtɹækt ˈfɔltɪ ˈmuvmɛnt baːɪ ɾɪˈplɛːɪsɪŋ ɪt wɪð æn ˈapozɪt ˈmoːʊʃʌn]

Exercise: [lɪp tɹɪl ʌ faːɪv toːʊn dɪˈsɛndɪŋ ænd ʌˈsɛndɪŋ skɛːɪl]

[ɹɛːɪz ðʌ hænd fɔ dɪˈsɛndɪŋ toːʊnz ænd ˈloːʊʌɾ ɪt fɔɾ ʌˈsɛndɪŋ toːʊnz]:

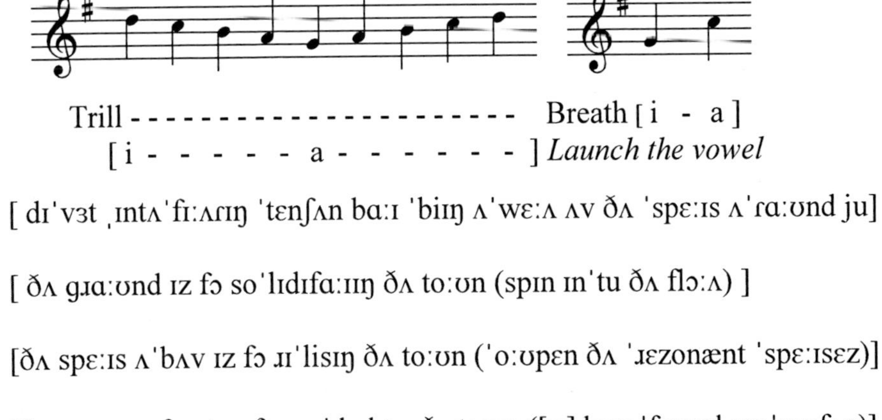

[dɪˈvɜt ˌɪntʌˈfɪːʌɾɪŋ ˈtɛnʃʌn baːɪ ˈbiɪŋ ʌˈwɛːʌ ʌv ðʌ ˈspɛːɪs ʌˈɹaːʊnd ju]

[ðʌ gɹaːʊnd ɪz fɔ soˈlɪdɪfaːɪɪŋ ðʌ toːʊn (spɪn ɪnˈtu ðʌ flɔːʌ)]

[ðʌ spɛːɪs ʌˈbʌv ɪz fɔ ɹɪˈlisɪŋ ðʌ toːʊn (ˈoːʊpɛn ðʌ ˈɹɛzonænt ˈspɛːɪsɛz)]

[ðʌ spɛːɪs ɪn fɹʌnt ɪz fɔ pɹoˈdʒɛktɪŋ ðʌ toːʊn ([æ] hæz ˈfɔwʊd sɛnˈsɛːɪʃʌn)]

Notes

Personal Assessment

Breath
Breath Control   70-------------79/80-------------89/90-------------100
Breath Expansion   70-------------79/80-------------89/90-------------100
Breath Support   70-------------79/80-------------89/90-------------100

Diction
Consonant Articulation 70-------------79/80-------------89/90-------------100
Vowel Formation   70-------------79/80-------------89/90-------------100

Musicianship
Expression   70-------------79/80-------------89/90-------------100
Legato   70-------------79/80-------------89/90-------------100
Pitch Accuracy   70-------------79/80-------------89/90-------------100
Rhythmic Accuracy   70-------------79/80-------------89/90-------------100

Posture and Tension
Postural Alignment   70-------------79/80-------------89/90-------------100
Release of Tension   70-------------79/80-------------89/90-------------100

Technique
Flexibility   70-------------79/80-------------89/90-------------100
Onset   70-------------79/80-------------89/90-------------100
Palatal Space   70-------------79/80-------------89/90-------------100
Pharyngeal Space   70-------------79/80-------------89/90-------------100
Projection   70-------------79/80-------------89/90-------------100
Vibrato   70-------------79/80-------------89/90-------------100
Tone Quality   70-------------79/80-------------89/90-------------100
Vowel Equalization   70-------------79/80-------------89/90-------------100

Remedy for Marking Tempo

[ˈsɪŋɪŋ ʃʊd bi smuð ænd kʌˈnɛktɛd (lɪˈgatoːʊ)]

[stʌˈkatoːʊ noːʊts ɑɾ ɑˈtɪkjulɛːɪtɛd wɪð ðʌ sʌˈpɔt nat ðʌ vɔːɪs]

[hɔɾɪˈzantʊl ˈmuvmɛnts ækˈsɛnʧuɛːɪt lɪˈgatoːʊ ˈsɪŋɪŋ]

[ˈvɜtɪkʊl ænd pɜˈkʌsɪv ˈmuvmɛnts dɪsˈɹʌpt lɪˈgatoːʊ ˈsɪŋɪŋ]

[ˈtæpɪŋ tu mak ðʌ bit ɪz ʌ ˈvɜtɪkʊl ænd pɜˈkʌsɪv ˈækʃʌn ʌv ðʌ fʊt]

[ˈplɛːɪŋ ðʌ ˈpjænoːʊ ɪz ʌ ˈvɜtɪkʊl ænd pɜˈkʌsɪv ˈækʃʌn ʌv ðʌ ˈfɪŋgʌz]

[ɹɪˈplɛːɪs ɛnɪ ˈvɜtɪkʊl ˈmuvmɛnt wɪð hɔɾɪˈzantʊl/lɪˈgatoːʊ ˈmuvmɛnt]

[plɛːɪ ði ɛːʌ ˈʧɛloːʊ swɪm θru ɛːʌɾ ɔ ˈpalɪʃ ðʌ ˈpjænoːʊ ʍaːɪl ˈsɪŋɪŋ]

Remedy for Rigidity and Shaking

[dɪsˈtɹækt ðʌ ˈfɔltɪ ˈmuvmɛnt baːɪ]:

1. [ˈbɛndɪŋ ðʌ niz ʍaːɪl ˈsɪŋɪŋ]

2. [ˈwɔkɪŋ ˈtɜnɪŋ ðʌ hɛd ɔ ˈmuvɪŋ ðʌ ʤɔ fɹʌm saːɪd tu saːɪd]

3. [ˈθroːʊɪŋ ʌ bɔl ɔ ˈflɪŋɪŋ ʌ ˈfɹɪzˈbi ʍaːɪl ˈsɪŋɪŋ]

Remedy for Inaccurate Formation

[laːɪt atɪkjuˈlɛːɪʃʌn hɛlps ʌˈvɔːɪd ɪntʌˈfɪːʌɾɪŋ ˈmʌskjulʌɾ ɪnˈtæŋgʊlmɛnts]

[ˈsɪmplɪfaːɪ ði ɑˈtɪkjulʌtɔɾɪ ˈpɹasɛs tu ʌˈvɔːɪd ɪksˈtɹɛːɪnɪʌs ˈmuvmɛnts]

[ˈfɜðʌ dɪsˈkʌʃʌn ɪz pɹoˈvaːɪdɛd ɪn ðʌ wik naːɪn ˈlɛsʌnz]

Notes

Personal Assessment

Breath
Breath Control   70-------------79/80-------------89/90-------------100
Breath Expansion   70-------------79/80-------------89/90-------------100
Breath Support   70-------------79/80-------------89/90-------------100

Diction
Consonant Articulation 70-------------79/80-------------89/90-------------100
Vowel Formation   70-------------79/80-------------89/90-------------100

Musicianship
Expression   70-------------79/80-------------89/90-------------100
Legato   70-------------79/80-------------89/90-------------100
Pitch Accuracy   70-------------79/80-------------89/90-------------100
Rhythmic Accuracy   70-------------79/80-------------89/90-------------100

Posture and Tension
Postural Alignment   70-------------79/80-------------89/90-------------100
Release of Tension   70-------------79/80-------------89/90-------------100

Technique
Flexibility   70-------------79/80-------------89/90-------------100
Onset   70-------------79/80-------------89/90-------------100
Palatal Space   70-------------79/80-------------89/90-------------100
Pharyngeal Space   70-------------79/80-------------89/90-------------100
Projection   70-------------79/80-------------89/90-------------100
Vibrato   70-------------79/80-------------89/90-------------100
Tone Quality   70-------------79/80-------------89/90-------------100
Vowel Equalization   70-------------79/80-------------89/90-------------100

Exploring Legato

[dɪsˈɹʌpʃʌnz ɪn ðʌ laːɪn hæv θɾi ˈpasɪbʊl ˈkɔzez]:

    1. [aˈtɪkjulɛːɪtɪŋ ðʌ toːʊn fɹʌm bɪˈloːʊ ænd ˈskupɪŋ ʌp]

    2. [aˈtɪkjulɛːɪtɪŋ ðʌ toːʊn wɪð ʌ ˈglatʊl stap (si pɛːɪʤ 59)]

    3. [aˈtɪkjulɛːɪtɪŋ ðʌ toːʊn wɪð ʌ [h] ˈansɛt]

[ˈnɛːɪzʊl [ŋ] ɪz æn ˈɛksɛlent lɪˈgatoːʊ tul]

[ɪt ˈɹɛzonɛːɪts ɪn ʌ spɛːɪs fa fɹʌm ðʌ ˈmɛkænɪzʌm ʌv ðʌ ˈglatʊl stap]

Legato Exercise

[ɹɪˈlis ðʌ ʤɔ ænd sɪŋ ʌ faːɪv toːʊn dɪˈsɛndɪŋ slaːɪd an [ŋ]]

[sɪŋ an ði ˈʌpʌ saːɪd ʌv ðʌ slaːɪd θɾuˈaːʊt ðʌ dɪˈsɛnt]

[ɪkˈsplɔːʌ ˈslaːɪdɪŋ θɾu æz ˈmɛnɪ ˈsɛmaːɪtoːʊnz æz ˈpasɪbʊl]

[ðɪs ˈækʃʌn ɹɪˈvilz sɛpʌˈɹɛːɪʃʌnz ðæt kɔz dɪsˈɹʌpʃʌnz ɪn ðʌ laːɪn]

[ɪt ɪz ˈkɾuʃʊl tu pɛːɪ ʌˈtɛnʃʌn tu ðʌ vɔːɪs bɪˈtwin ðʌ pɪʧ ˈʧɛːɪnʤɛz]

[ɹɪˈpit ðʌ skɛːɪl ˈslaːɪdɪŋ θɾu toːʊnz ʤʌst ʌˈbʌv ðʌ ˈlændɪŋ ˈpɪʧez]

[sɪŋ ðʌ skɛːɪl wɪðˈaːʊt slaːɪdz – toːʊnz ʃʊd ˈpɪvʌt fɹʌm pɪʧ tu pɪʧ]

Notes

Personal Assessment

Breath

Breath Control	70-------------79/80-------------89/90-------------100
Breath Expansion	70-------------79/80-------------89/90-------------100
Breath Support	70-------------79/80-------------89/90-------------100

Diction

Consonant Articulation	70-------------79/80-------------89/90-------------100
Vowel Formation	70-------------79/80-------------89/90-------------100

Musicianship

Expression	70-------------79/80-------------89/90-------------100
Legato	70-------------79/80-------------89/90-------------100
Pitch Accuracy	70-------------79/80-------------89/90-------------100
Rhythmic Accuracy	70-------------79/80-------------89/90-------------100

Posture and Tension

Postural Alignment	70-------------79/80-------------89/90-------------100
Release of Tension	70-------------79/80-------------89/90-------------100

Technique

Flexibility	70-------------79/80-------------89/90-------------100
Onset	70-------------79/80-------------89/90-------------100
Palatal Space	70-------------79/80-------------89/90-------------100
Pharyngeal Space	70-------------79/80-------------89/90-------------100
Projection	70-------------79/80-------------89/90-------------100
Vibrato	70-------------79/80-------------89/90-------------100
Tone Quality	70-------------79/80-------------89/90-------------100
Vowel Equalization	70-------------79/80-------------89/90-------------100

Advanced Exercise: Incorporating Vibrato

[sɪŋ æn ɪnˈtɛnslɪ ˈspɪnɪŋ [ŋ] ðæt ˈɹɛzoˌnɛːɪts ɪkˈsklusɪvlɪ ɪn ðʌ noːʊz]

[sɪŋ ðʌ [ŋ] wɪð slaːɪdz ænd mɛːɪnˈtɛːɪn ðʌ vaːɪˈbɹatoːʊ θɹu ɪtʃ slaːɪd]:

[ŋ] vibrato and slides

[sɪŋ ðʌ skɛːɪl wɪðˈaːʊt slaːɪdz]

[ðʌ toːʊnz ˈpɪvʌt fɹʌm pɪtʃ tu pɪtʃ ɪn æn ʌnɪntʌˈɹʌptɛd floːʊ ʌv saːʊnd]

[ðʌ spɪn ʃʊd ɪgˈzɪst wɪð ˈsɪŋgjulʌ ˈvaːɪbɹænsɪ θɹuˈaːʊt ðʌ skɛːɪl]

Adding the [a] Vowel

[juz ðʌ ˈfaloːʊɪŋ ˈɛksʌsaːɪz tu ˈɹɛplɪkɛːɪt ðʌ spɪn an æn [a] ˈvaːʊʌl]

[ðʌ spɛːɪs ʌv [a] hæz ʌ haːɪ ˈpælæt ænd ʌ loːʊ tʌŋ]

[ðʌ tʌŋ tɪp mʌst ˈɔlwɛːɪz tʌtʃ ðʌ ˈloːʊʌ fɹʌnt tiθ]

[mɛːɪnˈtɛːɪn ðʌ sɛːɪm ɹɪˈlist dʒɔ poˈzɪʃʌn fɔ ði ɪnˈtaːɪʌ ˈɛksʌsaːɪz]

[ðʌ [ŋ] ɪz mʌtʃ ˈsaftʌ ðæn ði [a] sɪns ðʌ [ŋ] spɛːɪs ɪz kʌnˈfaːɪnd]

[ɪnˈhans spɛːɪs baːɪ ˈplɛːɪsɪŋ ðʌ tʌŋ tɪp ˈʌpsaːɪd daːʊn an maːʊθ flɔːʌ]

Maintain Spin Throughout

Formation of [i]

Speaker's [i]

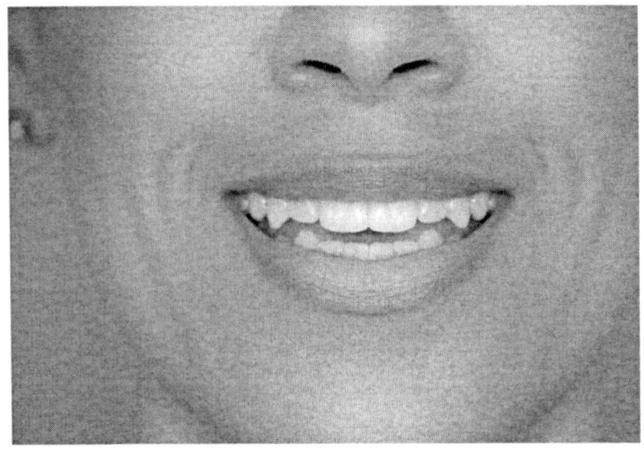

The [i] for speech is formed with the lips.

Singer's [i]

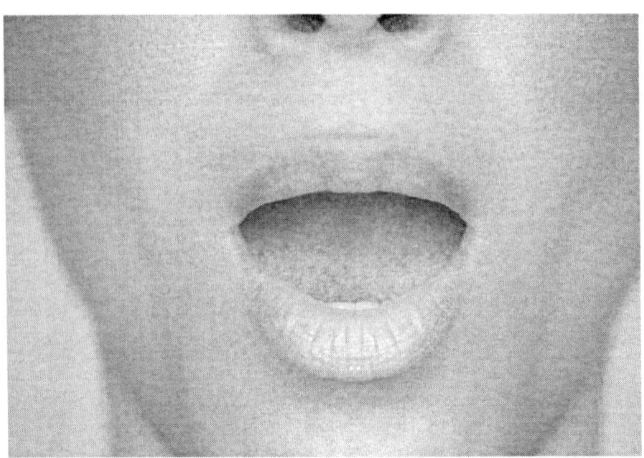

The [i] for singing is formed with the tongue. The jaw is released and the tongue arch is far forward.

Pharyngeal Space and the Breath: Week 5

Day 1: Exploring Pharyngeal Space – [i]

Day 2: Onsets and Legato – [j]

Day 3: Sensory Awareness

Day 4: Consonant Voicing and the Fricatives

Day 5: Breath Support

Day 6: Breath Control

Lesson Notes, Date: _____________

Checklist of Concepts to Review

BREATH
Breath Control___
p: 35, 63, 67
Breath Support___
p: 63, 65
Breath Expansion___
p: 33, 35
DICTION
Articulation___
p: 121, 123, 125, 131
Front Vowels___
p: 57, 105
Back Vowels___
p: 73, 107
Central Vowels___
p: 89, 91, 93, 109, 111
Mixed Vowels___
p: 113, 115
FLEXIBILITY
Flexibility___
p: 109, 139
MUSICIANSHIP
Artistry___
p: 141
Dynamics___
p: 143
Legato___
p: 49, 59, 75, 139, 141

POSTURE
Postural Alignment___
p: 25, 27
RANGE
Range___
p: 81, 91, 139
TONE
Chiaroscuro___
p: 97, 113, 115
Lip Trills___
p: 41, 43
Palatal Resonance___
p: 89, 91, 93, 109
Pharyngeal Space___
p: 57, 59, 93, 105, 109
Projection___
p: 73, 75, 93, 107
Register___
p: 43, 83
Resonance___
p: 93, 95, 97, 109, 137
Sensory Awareness___
p: 61, 127
Vibrato___
p: 43, 45, 51, 77, 79, 81
Vowel Equalization___
p: 79, 95, 137
WARM-UPS___
p: 200-204

WARNINGS
Breathy Tone___
p: 35, 77, 113, 125, 127
Faulty Formation___
p. 111, 127
Faulty Movement___
p. 45, 47
Faulty Onset___
p: 59, 75, 127
Jaw Tension___
p: 31, 111, 121, 123, 125
Nasal Tone ___
p: 111, 127
Pressed Tone___
p: 35, 41, 43, 83
Spread Tone___
p: 57, 61, 73, 111
Tension___
p: 29, 31, 45, 47, 61
Tongue Impeded Tone___
p: 111, 127
OTHER
Choral Singing___
p: 99
Stage Deportment___
p: 145
Vocal health___
p: 147

Daily Notes and Practice Times

Day 1   Practice Time:___________

Day 2   Practice Time:___________

Day 3   Practice Time:___________

Day 4   Practice Time:___________

Day 5   Practice Time:___________

Day 6   Practice Time:___________

Notes

Personal Assessment

Breath
Breath Control   70-------------79/80-------------89/90-------------100
Breath Expansion   70-------------79/80-------------89/90-------------100
Breath Support   70-------------79/80-------------89/90-------------100

Diction
Consonant Articulation 70-------------79/80-------------89/90-------------100
Vowel Formation   70-------------79/80-------------89/90-------------100

Musicianship
Expression   70-------------79/80-------------89/90-------------100
Legato   70-------------79/80-------------89/90-------------100
Pitch Accuracy   70-------------79/80-------------89/90-------------100
Rhythmic Accuracy   70-------------79/80-------------89/90-------------100

Posture and Tension
Postural Alignment   70-------------79/80-------------89/90-------------100
Release of Tension   70-------------79/80-------------89/90-------------100

Technique
Flexibility   70-------------79/80-------------89/90-------------100
Onset   70-------------79/80-------------89/90-------------100
Palatal Space   70-------------79/80-------------89/90-------------100
Pharyngeal Space   70-------------79/80-------------89/90-------------100
Projection   70-------------79/80-------------89/90-------------100
Vibrato   70-------------79/80-------------89/90-------------100
Tone Quality   70-------------79/80-------------89/90-------------100
Vowel Equalization   70-------------79/80-------------89/90-------------100

Exploring Pharyngeal Space – [i]
(see image on page 52)

[ði [i] fɔ spiʧ ɪz fɔmd baːɹ ˈspɹɛdɪŋ ðʌ lɪps]

[ði [i] fɔ ˈsɪŋɪŋ ɪz fɔmd wɪð ʌ ˈfɔwʊd aʧ ʌv ðʌ tʌŋ]

[fʌˈɹɪndʒʊl spɛːɪs ɪz ɪnˈkɹist ʍɛn ðʌ bʌlk ʌv ðʌ tʌŋ ɪz ˈfɔwʊd]

Tongue Push-Ups

[tʌŋ aʧ ˈɛksʌsaːɪzɛz ɹɪˈpɹoːʊgɹæm ðʌ spiʧ ˈmʌsʊlz fɔ ˈsɪŋɪŋ]

1. [ɹɪˈlis ðʌ dʒɔ fɔ [a] ænd ɹɛːɪz ðʌ saft ˈpælæt]

2. [ðʌ tʌŋ laːɪz loːʊ ænd flæt an ðʌ flɔːʌɾ ʌv ðʌ maːʊθ]

3. [ðʌ tʌŋ tɪp ˈkantækts ðʌ ˈloːʊʌ fɹʌnt tiθ fɔ ði ɪnˈtaːɪʌ ˈɛksʌsaːɪz]

4. [ðʌ lɪps ɑ ˈnaːɪðʌ ˈɹaːʊndɛd nɔ spɹɛd]

5. [fɔm [i] baːɪ ˈaʧɪŋ ðʌ tʌŋ ˈfɔwʊd (ʌbˈzɜv ɪn ʌ ˈmɪɹɔ)]

6. [ðʌ saːɪdz ʌv ðʌ tʌŋ ˈkantækt ðʌ lɛŋθ ʌv ði ˈʌpʌ ˈmoːʊlʌz]

7. [du nat spɹɛd ðʌ lɪps nɔ ˈɔltʌ ðʌ poˈzɪʃʌn ʌv ðʌ dʒɔ]

8. [ʧɛk fɔ ˈækjʊɹæsɪ baːɪ ˈʍɪspʌɹɪŋ æn [i] ˈvaːʊʌl]

9. [ˈɹɛkɔd ðʌ saːʊnd tu ɪnˈʃʊːʌ ðæt ɪt ɪz ˈækʧuʊlɪ [i] ænd nat [ɪ]]

10. [ɪf ˈvaːʊʌl ˈklæɹɪtɪ ɪz ˈlækɪŋ ɹˈnʌnsiɛːɪt [i] wɪð ʌ [j] tʌŋ aʧ]

11. [ˈɔltʌˌnɛːɪt bɹˈtwin [a] ænd [i] baːɪ minz ʌv tʌŋ ˈmuvmɛnt ˈoːʊnlɪ]

12. [mɛːɪnˈtɛːɪn ði [a] lɪp ænd dʒɔ poˈzɪʃʌn]

Notes

Personal Assessment

Breath

Breath Control   70--------------79/80--------------89/90--------------100
Breath Expansion   70--------------79/80--------------89/90--------------100
Breath Support   70--------------79/80--------------89/90--------------100

Diction

Consonant Articulation 70--------------79/80--------------89/90--------------100
Vowel Formation   70--------------79/80--------------89/90--------------100

Musicianship

Expression   70--------------79/80--------------89/90--------------100
Legato   70--------------79/80--------------89/90--------------100
Pitch Accuracy   70--------------79/80--------------89/90--------------100
Rhythmic Accuracy   70--------------79/80--------------89/90--------------100

Posture and Tension

Postural Alignment   70--------------79/80--------------89/90--------------100
Release of Tension   70--------------79/80--------------89/90--------------100

Technique

Flexibility   70--------------79/80--------------89/90--------------100
Onset   70--------------79/80--------------89/90--------------100
Palatal Space   70--------------79/80--------------89/90--------------100
Pharyngeal Space   70--------------79/80--------------89/90--------------100
Projection   70--------------79/80--------------89/90--------------100
Vibrato   70--------------79/80--------------89/90--------------100
Tone Quality   70--------------79/80--------------89/90--------------100
Vowel Equalization   70--------------79/80--------------89/90--------------100

Onsets – [j] Glide

[ʌ ˈglatʊl stap [ʔ] pɹɪˈsidz ði ˈansɛt ʌv ʌ ˈvaːʊʌl fɔ spiʧ]

[ðɪs pɜˈkʌsɪv gɹʌnt saːʊnd mʌst bi ʌˈvɔːɪdɛd fɔ ˈsɪŋɪŋ]

[ɹɪˈplɛːɪs ðʌ ˈfɔltɪ ˈansɛt ʌv ʌ fɹʌnt ˈvaːʊʌl wɪð ʌ ˈsaːɪlɛnt [j] glaːɪd]

[ʌ [j] glaːɪd ɪz ʌ ˈɹæpɪdlɪ aˈtɪkjulɛːɪtɛd [i]]

Legato – [j] Glide

[ˈglatʊl [ʔ] ænd [h] atɪkjuˈlɛːɪʃʌnz ɪntʌˈɹʌpt lɪˈgatoːʊ ˈmuvmɛnt]

[ðʌ [j] glaːɪd ɪz juzd tu ɹɪˈplɛːɪs saːʊndz ðæt dɪsˈɹʌpt ðʌ lɪˈgatoːʊ]

Sirens (Slides) – [j] Glide

[kʌˈmandz fɹʌm ðʌ maːɪnd tu ðʌ ˈbadɪ mʌst bi ˈkɛːʌfʊlɪ ʌbˈzɜvd]

[ðʌ maːɪnd mɛːɪ sɛnd ʌ kʌˈmand tu ɪnˈgɛːɪʤ ɪntʌˈfɪːʌrɪŋ ˈmʌsʊl grups]

[ʍat ˈmʌsʊl grups a toːʊld tu ɪnˈgɛːɪʤ ʍɛn ju pɹɪˈpɛːʌ tu sɪŋ]?

[ˈtɛnʃʌn ʌˈkɜz ʍɛn ˈmʌsʊlz ɹɪˈspand tu ʌ pʊːʌ kʌˈmand]

[ɹɪˈplɛːɪs ʌ ˈfɔltɪ ˈansɛt wɪð ʌ slaːɪd ɪn ˈɔdʌ tu ɪntʌˈɹʌpt ðʌ ˈpɹasɛs]

[ʌbˈzɜv jɔːʌ maːɪnd tu ˈmʌsʊl kʌˈmandz æz ju sɪŋ ðʌ ˈfaloːʊɪŋ]:

Notes

Personal Assessment

Breath

Breath Control   70-------------79/80-------------89/90-------------100
Breath Expansion   70-------------79/80-------------89/90-------------100
Breath Support   70-------------79/80-------------89/90-------------100

Diction

Consonant Articulation 70-------------79/80-------------89/90-------------100
Vowel Formation   70-------------79/80-------------89/90-------------100

Musicianship

Expression   70-------------79/80-------------89/90-------------100
Legato   70-------------79/80-------------89/90-------------100
Pitch Accuracy   70-------------79/80-------------89/90-------------100
Rhythmic Accuracy   70-------------79/80-------------89/90-------------100

Posture and Tension

Postural Alignment   70-------------79/80-------------89/90-------------100
Release of Tension   70-------------79/80-------------89/90-------------100

Technique

Flexibility   70-------------79/80-------------89/90-------------100
Onset   70-------------79/80-------------89/90-------------100
Palatal Space   70-------------79/80-------------89/90-------------100
Pharyngeal Space   70-------------79/80-------------89/90-------------100
Projection   70-------------79/80-------------89/90-------------100
Vibrato   70-------------79/80-------------89/90-------------100
Tone Quality   70-------------79/80-------------89/90-------------100
Vowel Equalization   70-------------79/80-------------89/90-------------100

Sensory Awareness

The resonance of a vibrant, well-projected tone is often described as having no sensation at all.

[ˈsɛnsɔɪɪ ʌˈwɛːʌnɛs ʌˈlaːʊz ðʌ ˈsɪŋʌ tu ʌbˈzɜv]:

1. [ˈpastʃʊɪʊl ʌˈlaːɪnmɛnt]   5. [ˈmʌskjulʌ ˈtɛnʃʌn]

2. [bɪɛθ ɪkˈspænʃʌn]   6. [ˈnɛːɪzʊl ˈɪɛzonæns]

3. [bɪɛθ sʌˈpɔt]   7. [ˈθɪoːʊtɪ toːʊn]

4. [ˈvaːʊʌl ænd ˈkansonænt fɔˈmɛːɪʃʌn]

[ˈsɛnsɔɪɪ ʌˈwɛːʌnɛs hɛlps ðʌ ˈsɪŋʌɪ ʌˈvɔːɪd pʊːʌ ˈvoːʊkʊl ˈhæbɪts]

The Pitfalls of Listening to Oneself While Singing

[ˈsɪŋʌz du nat ˈbɛnɛfɪt fɪʌm ˈlɪsɛnɪŋ tu ðɛmˈsɛlvz ʍaːɪl ˈsɪŋɪŋ]

[ðʌ ˈsɪŋʌɪ ɪz nat ˈlaːɪklɪ tu hɪːʌɪ ʌ ˈfɔltɪ toːʊn]

[ðɛːʌɪ a fɔːʌ wɛːɪz ˈlɪsɛnɪŋ kæn ɪmˈpid ðʌ ˈsɪŋɪŋ ˈpɪasɛs]:

1. [ˈlɪsɛnɪŋ ˈkɔzɛz ðʌ ˈsɪŋʌ tu læg bɪˈhaːɪnd ðʌ bit]

2. [æn ˈækjʊɪætlɪ fɔmd [i] ˈafɛn saːʊndz ʃɪɪl tu ðʌ ˈsɪŋʌ]

3. [ʌ ˈnɛːɪzʊl toːʊn mɛːɪ saːʊnd wɛl pɪoˈdʒɛktɛd tu ðʌ ˈsɪŋʌ]

4. [ʌ ˈkʌvʌd toːʊn mɛːɪ saːʊnd ˈɪɛzonænt tu ðʌ ˈsɪŋʌ]

Block the area in front of your ears with folders while you sing so that you can experience your sound from an alternate direction. It is always best to observe feeling rather than sound while singing.

Notes

Personal Assessment

Breath

Breath Control   70-------------79/80-------------89/90-------------100
Breath Expansion   70-------------79/80-------------89/90-------------100
Breath Support   70-------------79/80-------------89/90-------------100

Diction

Consonant Articulation 70-------------79/80-------------89/90-------------100
Vowel Formation   70-------------79/80-------------89/90-------------100

Musicianship

Expression   70-------------79/80-------------89/90-------------100
Legato   70-------------79/80-------------89/90-------------100
Pitch Accuracy   70-------------79/80-------------89/90-------------100
Rhythmic Accuracy   70-------------79/80-------------89/90-------------100

Posture and Tension

Postural Alignment   70-------------79/80-------------89/90-------------100
Release of Tension   70-------------79/80-------------89/90-------------100

Technique

Flexibility   70-------------79/80-------------89/90-------------100
Onset   70-------------79/80-------------89/90-------------100
Palatal Space   70-------------79/80-------------89/90-------------100
Pharyngeal Space   70-------------79/80-------------89/90-------------100
Projection   70-------------79/80-------------89/90-------------100
Vibrato   70-------------79/80-------------89/90-------------100
Tone Quality   70-------------79/80-------------89/90-------------100
Vowel Equalization   70-------------79/80-------------89/90-------------100

Consonant Voicing

[ʌ vɔːɪst ˈkansonænt kæn bi sʌŋ]

[ʌ ˈvɔːɪsləs ˈkansonænt kæn ˈoːʊnlɪ bi ˈʍɪspʌd]

[ðʌ vaːɹˈbɹɛːɪʃʌn ʌv ʌ vɔːɪst ˈkansonænt mɛːɪ bi fɛlt baːɹ ˈtʌʧɪŋ ðʌ θɾoːʊt]

[ðʌ ˈfaloːʊɪŋ vɔːɪst ænd ˈvɔːɪsləs pɛːʌz ʃɛːʌ ðʌ sɛːɪm fɔˈmɛːɪʃʌn]:

[b]/[p]; [d]/[t]; [w]/[ʍ]; [ʤ]/[ʧ]; [g]/[k]

[ʌbˈzɜv ˈvɔːɪsɪŋ baːɹ ˈtʌʧɪŋ ðʌ θɾoːʊt ˈdjʊːʌɾɪŋ atɪkjuˈlɛːɪʃʌn]

Fricatives

[bɹɛθ floːʊz past ʌ kʌnˈstɹɪktɛd ˈpæsæʤwɛːɪ fɔ ˈfɹɪkʌtɪv ˈkansonænts]

[ˈʤɛntʊl ˈkantækt ˈaptɪmaːɪzɛz ðʌ ˈvaːɪbɹænsɪ ʌv ˈfɹɪkʌtɪvz]

[pɹɛst ˈkantækt staps ði ɛːʌ floːʊ ænd ˈmʌfʊlz ðʌ saːʊnd]

[ðʌ vɔːɪst ˈfɹɪkʌtɪvz hæv ˈvɔːɪsləs ˈkaːʊntʌpats]:

<table>
<tr><td></td><td></td><td>Voiced</td><td>Voiceless</td><td></td></tr>
<tr><td></td><td rowspan="4">{</td><td>[ð]</td><td>[θ]</td><td rowspan="4">}</td></tr>
<tr><td>Breath</td><td>[v]</td><td>[f]</td><td>Breath</td></tr>
<tr><td>Support</td><td>[z]</td><td>[s]</td><td>Control</td></tr>
<tr><td></td><td>[ʒ]</td><td>[ʃ]</td><td></td></tr>
</table>

[aˈtɪkjulɛːɪt ænd sʌˈstɛːɪn ðʌ vɔːɪst ˈfɹɪkʌtɪvz ɪn ðʌ ˈfaloːʊɪŋ ˈmænʌ]:

[ɪnˈhɛːɪl æn [a] an 7 kaːʊnts ænd ɛksˈhɛːɪl ʌ vɔːɪst ˈfɹɪkʌtɪv an 7 kaːʊnts]

[ˈgɹæʤuʊlɪ ˈlaːɪtɛn ðʌ ˈkantækt ʌnˈtɪl ˈaptɪmʊl ˈvaːɪbɹænsɪ ɪz ʌˈʧivd]

[juz ˈfɹɪkʌtɪvz tu dɪsˈkʌvʌ bɹɛθ sʌˈpɔt ænd ˈmanɪtʌ bɹɛθ kʌnˈtɹoːʊl]

Notes

Personal Assessment

Breath
Breath Control   70-------------79/80-------------89/90-------------100
Breath Expansion   70-------------79/80-------------89/90-------------100
Breath Support   70-------------79/80-------------89/90-------------100

Diction
Consonant Articulation 70-------------79/80-------------89/90-------------100
Vowel Formation   70-------------79/80-------------89/90-------------100

Musicianship
Expression   70-------------79/80-------------89/90-------------100
Legato   70-------------79/80-------------89/90-------------100
Pitch Accuracy   70-------------79/80-------------89/90-------------100
Rhythmic Accuracy   70-------------79/80-------------89/90-------------100

Posture and Tension
Postural Alignment   70-------------79/80-------------89/90-------------100
Release of Tension   70-------------79/80-------------89/90-------------100

Technique
Flexibility   70-------------79/80-------------89/90-------------100
Onset   70-------------79/80-------------89/90-------------100
Palatal Space   70-------------79/80-------------89/90-------------100
Pharyngeal Space   70-------------79/80-------------89/90-------------100
Projection   70-------------79/80-------------89/90-------------100
Vibrato   70-------------79/80-------------89/90-------------100
Tone Quality   70-------------79/80-------------89/90-------------100
Vowel Equalization   70-------------79/80-------------89/90-------------100

Breath Support

[bɹɛθ sʌˈpɔt ɹɪˈkwaːɪɑz mʌltɪˈtaskɪŋ ænd ʌ spɪˈsɪfɪk ˈɔdɑɾ ʌv apʌˈɾɛːɪʃʌnz]

Review

[ɹɪˈpit ðiz stɛps tu dɪsˈkʌvʌ ðʌ loːʊ sʌˈpɔt ˈnidɛd fɔ ˈsɪŋɪŋ]:

1. [ɪˈstæblɪʃ æn ˈɛnʌʤaːɪzd ˈpasʧʊɾʊl ʌˈlaːɪnmɛnt]

2. [ɪkˈspænd loːʊ fɔ ðʌ bɹɛθ]

3. [mɛːɪnˈtɛːɪn ðʌ ˈʤɛsʧʊɾ ʌv ɪnhʌˈlɛːɪʃʌn baːɪ ɾɪˈlisɪŋ ðʌ ɹɪb kɛːɪʤ]

4. [ɪnˈgɛːɪʤ ðʌ sʌˈpɔt ʍaːɪl ˈsɪŋɪŋ]

[ðʌ ˈloːʊʌ ˈæbdomɛn ɪz ˈæktɪv ʍaːɪl ðʌ ˈstɜnʌm ænd ɹɪbz ɹɪˈmɛːɪn stɪl]

[ɪnˈgɛːɪʤ ðʌ sʌˈpɔt fɔ ɪʧ aˈtɪkjulɛːɪʃʌn ʌv ðʌ ˈfaloːʊɪŋ]:

[kʌˈnɛkt ði ˈɑnsɛt ʌv ðʌ [z] wɪð ðʌ ˈloːʊʌ ˈæbdomɛn]

Repeat the exercise above and sustain the last [zi]. Release and support the breath three times while sustaining the vowel. Observe the low release and use of the breath while sustaining the tone.

[ɹɪˈvju ðʌ fɔˈmɛːɪʃʌn ʌv [i] ænd sɪŋ ðʌ ˈfaloːʊɪŋ]:

Support
Exercise:

Notes

Personal Assessment

Breath
Breath Control   70-------------79/80-------------89/90-------------100
Breath Expansion   70-------------79/80-------------89/90-------------100
Breath Support   70-------------79/80-------------89/90-------------100

Diction
Consonant Articulation 70-------------79/80-------------89/90-------------100
Vowel Formation   70-------------79/80-------------89/90-------------100

Musicianship
Expression   70-------------79/80-------------89/90-------------100
Legato   70-------------79/80-------------89/90-------------100
Pitch Accuracy   70-------------79/80-------------89/90-------------100
Rhythmic Accuracy   70-------------79/80-------------89/90-------------100

Posture and Tension
Postural Alignment   70-------------79/80-------------89/90-------------100
Release of Tension   70-------------79/80-------------89/90-------------100

Technique
Flexibility   70-------------79/80-------------89/90-------------100
Onset   70-------------79/80-------------89/90-------------100
Palatal Space   70-------------79/80-------------89/90-------------100
Pharyngeal Space   70-------------79/80-------------89/90-------------100
Projection   70-------------79/80-------------89/90-------------100
Vibrato   70-------------79/80-------------89/90-------------100
Tone Quality   70-------------79/80-------------89/90-------------100
Vowel Equalization   70-------------79/80-------------89/90-------------100

Breath Control

Breath is tone. Barbara Honn

[bɹɛθ sʌˈpɔt ɪz ði ɪnˈgɛːɪdʒmɛnt ʌv ðʌ bɹɛθ]

[bɹɛθ kʌnˈtɹoːʊl ɪz ði ɪˈfɪʃɛnt ɹɪˈlis ʌv ðʌ bɹɛθ (si pɛːɪdʒ ˈθ3tɪfaːɪv)]

[ðʌ ˈvɔːɪslɛs ˈfɹɪkʌtɪvz kæn bi juzd tu tɛst bɹɛθ ɪˈfɪʃɛnsɪ]

Warnings

[du nat ɪnˈhɛːɪl mɔːʌ ɛːʌ ðæn ɪz ˈnidɛd fɔ ðʌ fɹɛːɪz]

[ʌ ˈnɔːɪzɪ ɪnhʌˈlɛːɪʃʌn ˈɪndɪkɛːɪts kʌnˈstɹɪkʃʌn ɪn ðʌ ˈvoːʊkʊl æpʌˈrætʌs]

[kʌnˈstɹɪkʃʌn ɪnˈhɪbɪts ði ɪˈfɪʃɛnt ɹɪˈlis ʌv ðʌ bɹɛθ]

Exercises

[ðɪz ˈɛksʌsaːɪzɛz hɛlp ˈstjudɛnts ˈmanɪtʌ ðʌ kʌnˈsɪstɛnsɪ ʌv ði ɛːʌ floːʊ]

[ɪnˈhɛːɪl æn [a] an ˈsɛvɛn kaːʊnts ænd ɛksˈhɛːɪl ʌ [s] an ˈsɛvɛn kaːʊnts]

[laːɪt ˈkantækt bɪˈtwin ði aˈtɪkjulɛːɪtɔz ʌˈlaːʊz ðʌ bɹɛθ tu floːʊ]

[mɛːɪnˈtɛːɪn ʌ kʌnˈsɪstɛnt ˈvɔːɪslɛs floːʊ ʌv ɛːʌr ænd ɹɪˈlis ɔl ðʌ bɹɛθ]

[ɹɪˈpit ði ˈɛksʌsaːɪz wɪð ɔl ˈvɔːɪslɛs ˈfɹɪkʌtɪvz [f] [s] [ʃ] [θ]]

[ɹɪˈpit ði ˈɛksʌsaːɪz ʌˈbʌv θɹu ʌ stɹɔ tu ˈɹɛplɪkɛːɪt ɪˈfɪʃɛnt ɛːʌ floːʊ]

Formation of [u]

Speaker's [u]

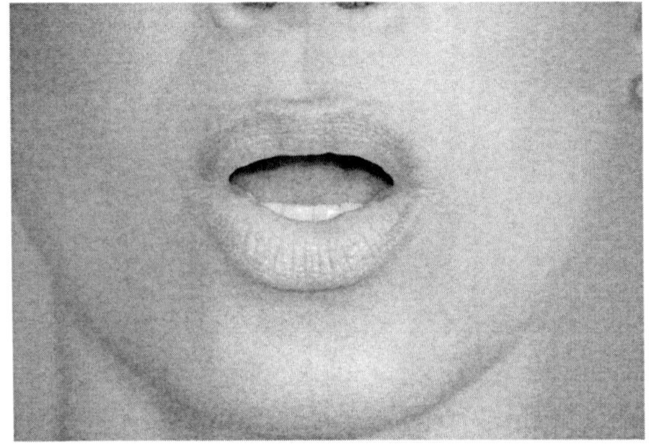

The closed back [u] formation is lax for speech.

Singer's [u]

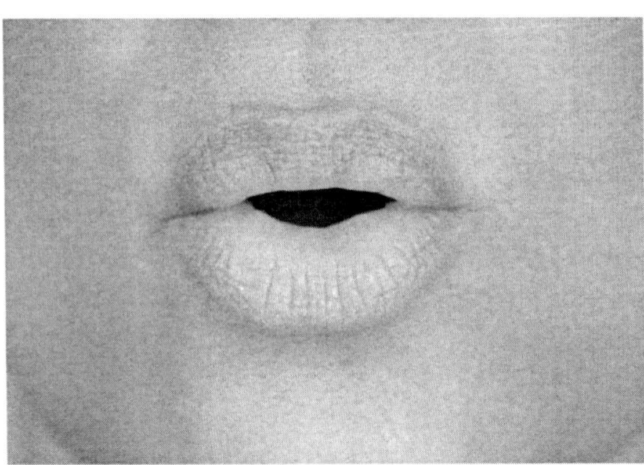

The [u] for singing requires a forward rounding of the lips initiated by the muscles in the cheeks. Avoid tensely rounded lips, outward curled lips, inward curled lips, pinched lip corners, or a weak lip rounding.

Projection and Vibrato: Week 6

Day 1: Exploring Projection of the Tone – [u]

Day 2: Onsets and Legato Connection – [w]

Day 3: Vibrato

Day 4: Head Voice Vibrato

Day 5: Support Vibrato

Day 6: Equalizing the Scale

Lesson Notes, Date: ___________

Checklist of Concepts to Review

BREATH
Breath Control___
p: 35, 63, 67
Breath Support___
p: 63, 65
Breath Expansion___
p: 33, 35
DICTION
Articulation___
p: 121, 123, 125, 131
Front Vowels___
p: 57, 105
Back Vowels___
p: 73, 107
Central Vowels___
p: 89, 91, 93, 109, 111
Mixed Vowels___
p: 113, 115
FLEXIBILITY
Flexibility___
p: 109, 139
MUSICIANSHIP
Artistry___
p: 141
Dynamics___
p: 143
Legato___
p: 49, 59, 75, 139, 141

POSTURE
Postural Alignment___
p: 25, 27
RANGE
Range___
p: 81, 91, 139
TONE
Chiaroscuro___
p: 97, 113, 115
Lip Trills___
p: 41, 43
Palatal Resonance___
p: 89, 91, 93, 109
Pharyngeal Space___
p: 57, 59, 93, 105, 109
Projection___
p: 73, 75, 93, 107
Register___
p: 43, 83
Resonance___
p: 93, 95, 97, 109, 137
Sensory Awareness___
p: 61, 127
Vibrato___
p: 43, 45, 51, 77, 79, 81
Vowel Equalization___
p: 79, 95, 137
WARM-UPS___
p: 200-204

WARNINGS
Breathy Tone___
p: 35, 77, 113, 125, 127
Faulty Formation___
p. 111, 127
Faulty Movement___
p. 45, 47
Faulty Onset___
p: 59, 75, 127
Jaw Tension___
p: 31, 111, 121, 123, 125
Nasal Tone___
p: 111, 127
Pressed Tone___
p: 35, 41, 43, 83
Spread Tone___
p: 57, 61, 73, 111
Tension___
p: 29, 31, 45, 47, 61
Tongue Impeded Tone___
p: 111, 127
OTHER
Choral Singing___
p: 99
Stage Deportment___
p: 145
Vocal health___
p: 147

Daily Notes and Practice Times

Day 1   Practice Time:__________

Day 2   Practice Time:__________

Day 3   Practice Time:__________

Day 4   Practice Time:__________

Day 5   Practice Time:__________

Day 6   Practice Time:__________

Notes

Personal Assessment

Breath
Breath Control	70-------------79/80--------------89/90-------------100
Breath Expansion	70-------------79/80--------------89/90-------------100
Breath Support	70-------------79/80--------------89/90-------------100

Diction
Consonant Articulation	70-------------79/80-------------89/90------------100
Vowel Formation	70-------------79/80-------------89/90------------100

Musicianship
Expression	70-------------79/80--------------89/90-------------100
Legato	70-------------79/80--------------89/90-------------100
Pitch Accuracy	70-------------79/80-------------89/90-------------100
Rhythmic Accuracy	70-------------79/80-------------89/90-------------100

Posture and Tension
Postural Alignment	70-------------79/80-------------89/90-------------100
Release of Tension	70-------------79/80-------------89/90-------------100

Technique
Flexibility	70-------------79/80--------------89/90-------------100
Onset	70-------------79/80-------------89/90------------100
Palatal Space	70---------------79/80-------------89/90------------100
Pharyngeal Space	70-------------79/80-------------89/90-------------100
Projection	70-------------79/80--------------89/90-------------100
Vibrato	70-------------79/80-------------89/90-------------100
Tone Quality	70-------------79/80-------------89/90------------100
Vowel Equalization	70-------------79/80-------------89/90------------100

Exploring Projection of the Tone – [u]
(see image on page 68)

[ðʌ ˈɹaːʊndɪŋ ʌv [u] fɔ spiʧ ɪz læks ænd fɔmd ˈdjuːʌrɪŋ aˈtɪkjuleːɪʃʌn]

[ði [u] fɔ ˈsɪŋɪŋ ɹɪˈkwaːɹʌz æn ˈɜlɪ ˈfɔwʊd ˈɹaːʊndɪŋ ʌv ðʌ lɪps]

[ʌ ˈfɔwʊd ˈɹaːʊndɪŋ ʌv ðʌ lɪps pɹoˈʤɛkts ðʌ toːʊn]

Lip Rounds

[lɪp ˈɹaːʊndɪŋ ˈɛksʌsaːɪzez ɹɪˈpɹoːʊgɹæm ðʌ spiʧ ˈmʌsʊlz fɔ ˈsɪŋɪŋ]

1. [ɹɪˈlis ðʌ ʤɔ fɔ [a] ænd ɹɛːɪz ðʌ saft ˈpælæt]

2. [ðʌ tʌŋ laːɪz loːʊ ænd flæt an ðʌ flɔːʌr ʌv ðʌ maːʊθ]

3. [ðʌ tʌŋ tɪp ˈkantækts ðʌ ˈloːʊʌ fɹʌnt tiθ fɔ ði ɪnˈtaːɪʌ ˈɛksʌsaːɪz]

4. [ðʌ lɪps a ˈnaːɪðʌ ˈɹaːʊndɛd nɔ spɹɛd]

5. [fɔm [u] wɪð ʌ ˈfɔwʊd ˈɹaːʊndɪŋ ʌv ðʌ lɪps (ʌbˈzɜv ɪn ʌ ˈmɪɹɔ)]

6. [fɔm [u] ˈɹæpɪdlɪ tu ʌˈvɔːɪd dɪfθaŋaːɪzˈɛːɪʃʌn]

7. [du nat ˈɔltʌ ðʌ ɹɪˈlist [a] poˈzɪʃʌn ʌv ðʌ ʤɔ]

8. [ʧɛk fɔ ˈækjʊræsɪ baːɪ ˈʍɪspʌrɪŋ æn [u] ˈvaːʊʌl]

9. [ˈɹɛkɔd ðʌ saːʊnd tu ɪnˈʃuːʌ ðæt ɪt ɪz ˈækʧuʊlɪ [u] ænd nat [ʌ]]

10. [ɪf ˈvaːʊʌl ˈklærɪtɪ ɪz ˈlækɪŋ ɪˈnʌnsɪɛːɪt [u] wɪð ʌ [w] fɔˈmɛːɪʃʌn]

11. [ˈɔltʌˌnɛːɪt bɪˈtwin [a] ænd [u] baːɪ minz ʌv lɪp ænd ʧik ˈmuvmɛnt]

12. [mɛːɪnˈtɛːɪn ði [a] ʤɔ poˈzɪʃʌn]

Notes

Personal Assessment

Breath
Breath Control   70-------------79/80-------------89/90-------------100
Breath Expansion   70-------------79/80-------------89/90-------------100
Breath Support   70-------------79/80-------------89/90-------------100

Diction
Consonant Articulation 70-------------79/80-------------89/90-------------100
Vowel Formation   70-------------79/80-------------89/90-------------100

Musicianship
Expression   70-------------79/80-------------89/90-------------100
Legato   70-------------79/80-------------89/90-------------100
Pitch Accuracy   70-------------79/80-------------89/90-------------100
Rhythmic Accuracy   70-------------79/80-------------89/90-------------100

Posture and Tension
Postural Alignment   70-------------79/80-------------89/90-------------100
Release of Tension   70-------------79/80-------------89/90-------------100

Technique
Flexibility   70-------------79/80-------------89/90-------------100
Onset   70-------------79/80-------------89/90-------------100
Palatal Space   70-------------79/80-------------89/90-------------100
Pharyngeal Space   70-------------79/80-------------89/90-------------100
Projection   70-------------79/80-------------89/90-------------100
Vibrato   70-------------79/80-------------89/90-------------100
Tone Quality   70-------------79/80-------------89/90-------------100
Vowel Equalization   70-------------79/80-------------89/90-------------100

Onsets – [w] Glide

[ʌ ˈglatʊl stap [ʔ] pɹɪˈsidz ði ˈanset ʌv ʌ ˈvaːʊʌl fɔ spitʃ]

[ðɪs pɜˈkʌsɪv gɹʌnt saːʊnd mʌst bi ʌˈvɔːɪdɛd fɔ ˈsɪŋɪŋ]

[ɹɪˈplɛːɪs ðʌ ˈfɔltɪ ˈanset ʌv ʌ bæk ˈvaːʊʌl wɪð ʌ ˈsaːɪlɛnt [w] glaːɪd]

[ʌ [w] glaːɪd ɪz ʌ ˈɹæpɪdlɪ aˈtɪkjulɛːɪtɛd [u]]

Legato – [w] Glide

[ˈglatʊl [ʔ] ænd [h] atɪkjuˈlɛːɪʃʌnz ɪntʌˈɹʌpt lɪˈgatoːʊ ˈmuvmɛnt]

[ðʌ [w] glaːɪd ɪz juzd tu ɹɪˈplɛːɪs saːʊndz ðæt dɪsˈɹʌpt ðʌ lɪˈgatoːʊ]

Sirens (Slides) – [w] Glide

[kʌˈmandz fɹʌm ðʌ maːɪnd tu ðʌ ˈbadɪ mʌst bi ˈkɛːʌfʊlɪ ʌbˈzɜvd]

[ˈtɛnʃʌn ʌˈkɜz ʍɛn ˈmʌsʊlz ɹɪˈspand tu ʌ pʊːʌ kʌˈmand]

[ɹɪˈplɛːɪs ʌ ˈfɔltɪ ˈanset wɪð ʌ slaːɪd ɪn ˈɔdʌ tu kɔˈɹɛkt ðʌ ˈpɹasɛs]

[ʌbˈzɜv jɔːʌ maːɪnd tu ˈmʌsʊl kʌˈmandz æz ju sɪŋ ðʌ ˈfaloːʊɪŋ]:

Mimicking

Sounds in nature provide excellent examples of non-glottal onsets, pure vowels, and well-projected tones: a dog's whine [n], an owl's hoot [hu], a cat's hiss [çi], or a cat's meow [mieɛjaɑɔoʊu].

Notes

Personal Assessment

Breath
Breath Control   70-------------79/80-------------89/90-------------100
Breath Expansion   70-------------79/80-------------89/90-------------100
Breath Support   70-------------79/80-------------89/90-------------100

Diction
Consonant Articulation 70-------------79/80-------------89/90-------------100
Vowel Formation   70-------------79/80-------------89/90-------------100

Musicianship
Expression   70-------------79/80-------------89/90-------------100
Legato   70-------------79/80-------------89/90-------------100
Pitch Accuracy   70-------------79/80-------------89/90-------------100
Rhythmic Accuracy   70-------------79/80-------------89/90-------------100

Posture and Tension
Postural Alignment   70-------------79/80-------------89/90-------------100
Release of Tension   70-------------79/80-------------89/90-------------100

Technique
Flexibility   70-------------79/80-------------89/90-------------100
Onset   70-------------79/80-------------89/90-------------100
Palatal Space   70-------------79/80-------------89/90-------------100
Pharyngeal Space   70-------------79/80-------------89/90-------------100
Projection   70-------------79/80-------------89/90-------------100
Vibrato   70-------------79/80-------------89/90-------------100
Tone Quality   70-------------79/80-------------89/90-------------100
Vowel Equalization   70-------------79/80-------------89/90-------------100

Vibrato

[ðʌ tɜm vɑːɪˈbɹatoːʊ meːɪ hæv ʌ ˈnɛgʌtɪv ˌkanoˈtɛːɪʃʌn]

[sʌm pɹɪˈfɜ tu kɔl ɪt ˈvɑːɪbɹænsɪ ˈʃɪmʌ ɔ spɪn]

Vibrato (or spin) is a vocalized mechanism of the air that can be conceptualized in various resonating chambers.

[vɑːɪˈbɹatoːʊ ɹɪˈkwɑːɪʌz bɹɛθ spɛːɪs ʌ ɹɪˈlist æpʌˈrætʌs ænd toːʊn]

Space

A student may have a lovely vibrato but actualize it in the wrong way.

[ðʌ ˈpʌlsɛz ʌv ɛːʌ (toːʊn) meːɪ sɑːʊnd æz ɪf ðɛːɪ ˈɛmæˌnɛːɪt fɹʌm]:

    1. [ðʌ noːʊz (ˈnɛːɪzʊl toːʊn – [ŋ])]

    2. [ðʌ θɾoːʊt (ˈbɹɛθɪ toːʊn – [h])]

    3. [ðʌ ˈvɑːʊʌl spɛːɪs (ˈvɑːɪbɹænt toːʊn)]

Released Vocal Apparatus

[vɑːɪˈbɹatoːʊ ɪz ɪnˈɪʃɪɛːɪtɛd ʍɛn ɛːʌ muvz past ʌ ɹɪˈlist æpʌˈrætʌs]

Tone

The vibrato is actualized when the voice is engaged and the appropriate resonant space is prepared. Vocalization of the vibrato is comparable to consonant voicing.

[ɪkˈsplɔːʌ vɔːɪst ænd ˈvɔːɪslɛs aˈtɪkjulɛːɪʃʌnz ʌv ðʌ ˈfaloːʊɪŋ]:

    Rolled "r"   Lip Trill   [h]/[a] (with vibrato)

Notes

Personal Assessment

Breath

Breath Control 70-------------79/80-------------89/90-------------100
Breath Expansion 70-------------79/80-------------89/90-------------100
Breath Support 70-------------79/80-------------89/90-------------100

Diction

Consonant Articulation 70-------------79/80-------------89/90-------------100
Vowel Formation 70-------------79/80-------------89/90-------------100

Musicianship

Expression 70-------------79/80-------------89/90-------------100
Legato 70-------------79/80-------------89/90-------------100
Pitch Accuracy 70-------------79/80-------------89/90-------------100
Rhythmic Accuracy 70-------------79/80-------------89/90-------------100

Posture and Tension

Postural Alignment 70-------------79/80-------------89/90-------------100
Release of Tension 70-------------79/80-------------89/90-------------100

Technique

Flexibility 70-------------79/80-------------89/90-------------100
Onset 70-------------79/80-------------89/90-------------100
Palatal Space 70-------------79/80-------------89/90-------------100
Pharyngeal Space 70-------------79/80-------------89/90-------------100
Projection 70-------------79/80-------------89/90-------------100
Vibrato 70-------------79/80-------------89/90-------------100
Tone Quality 70-------------79/80-------------89/90-------------100
Vowel Equalization 70-------------79/80-------------89/90-------------100

Head Voice Vibrato

[ˈneːɪzʊl ˈkansonænts a ˈɛksɛlɛnt fɔɾ ɪkˈsplɔːʌɾɪŋ vaːɪˈbɹatoːʊ]

[ðʌ bɹɛθ ɪz ɹɪˈlist wɪðˈɪn ʌ dɪˈfaːɪnʌbʊl speːɪs fɔɾ ʌ ˈspɪnɪŋ [ŋ] toːʊn]

[kloːʊzd ˈvaːʊʌlz ˈɔlsoːʊ pɹoˈvaːɪd ʌ dɪˈfaːɪnʌbʊl speːɪs fɔ vaːɪˈbɹatoːʊ]

[ði [u] ænd [y] ˈvaːʊʌlz a ðʌ moːʊst ˈɹaːʊndɛd ʌv ɔl ðʌ ˈvaːʊʌlz]

[ði [i] ænd [y] ˈvaːʊʌlz hæv ðʌ moːʊst ˈfɹʌntɛd tʌŋ ʌv ɔl ðʌ ˈvaːʊʌlz]

Most singers find it easiest to discover vibrato in the clearly defined space of a closed [u] *or* [i] *formation. Some singers find it easier to discover vibrancy (or vibrato) in the* [a], [ɑ], *or* [ɔ] *space. It is important to discover your optimal vowel and proceed from there.*

[juz ðʌ ˈfaloːʊɪŋ ˈɛksʌsaːɪzɛz tu ɪkˈsplɔːʌ vaːɪˈbɹatoːʊ ænd ˈvaːʊʌl speːɪs]

[ʍɪtʃ ˈvaːʊʌl pɹoˈvaːɪdz ði ˈaptɪmʊl ɹɪˈlis ʌv ðʌ vaːɪˈbɹatoːʊ fɔ ju]?

[u — — — — — — — — — —]   Record Observations:
[i — — — — — — — — — —]   ___________________
[a — — — — — — — — — —]   ___________________
[ɑ — — — — — — — — — —]   ___________________
[ɔ — — — — — — — — — —]   ___________________

[ˈɔltʌneːɪt bɪˈtwin ðʌ ˈvaːʊʌlz tu dɪsˈkʌvʌ ˈikwʊlaːɪzd ˈvaːɪbɹænsɪ]:

~ *George Bitzas*

Notes

Personal Assessment

Breath

Breath Control   70-------------79/80-------------89/90-------------100
Breath Expansion   70-------------79/80-------------89/90-------------100
Breath Support   70-------------79/80-------------89/90-------------100

Diction

Consonant Articulation 70-------------79/80-------------89/90-------------100
Vowel Formation   70-------------79/80-------------89/90-------------100

Musicianship

Expression   70-------------79/80-------------89/90-------------100
Legato   70-------------79/80-------------89/90-------------100
Pitch Accuracy   70-------------79/80-------------89/90-------------100
Rhythmic Accuracy   70-------------79/80-------------89/90-------------100

Posture and Tension

Postural Alignment   70-------------79/80-------------89/90-------------100
Release of Tension   70-------------79/80-------------89/90-------------100

Technique

Flexibility   70-------------79/80-------------89/90-------------100
Onset   70-------------79/80-------------89/90-------------100
Palatal Space   70-------------79/80-------------89/90-------------100
Pharyngeal Space   70-------------79/80-------------89/90-------------100
Projection   70-------------79/80-------------89/90-------------100
Vibrato   70-------------79/80-------------89/90-------------100
Tone Quality   70-------------79/80-------------89/90-------------100
Vowel Equalization   70-------------79/80-------------89/90-------------100

Support Vibrato

When the mechanism of vibrato is conceptualized in the lower abdomen, the tone is supported, thus the term "support vibrato".

When the mechanism of vibrato is conceptualized in the clarity of the vowel, the tone is focused, thus the term "head voice vibrato".

The optimal approach is to produce support and head voice vibrato simultaneously and maintain a careful balance of the two.

Support Vibrato Exercise

[sɪŋ ðʌ ˈfaloːʊɪŋ ˈɛksʌsaːɪz ɪn ʌ ˈloːʊʌ ɹɛːɪndʒ ʌv ðʌ vɔːɪs]:

Expand low for each breath, then support and spin the [i] vowel.

Support and Head Voice Vibrato Exercises

[sʌˈpɔt ænd hɛd vɔːɪs vaːɪˈbɹatoːʊ ɑ kʌmˈbaːɪnd ɪn ðiz ˈɛksʌsaːɪzɛz]

[juz ðʌ sʌˈpɔt (<u>nat ˈplɛːɪsmɛnt</u>) ʌv ðʌ loːʊ noːʊt tu sɪŋ ði ˈaktɪv ʌˈbʌv]:

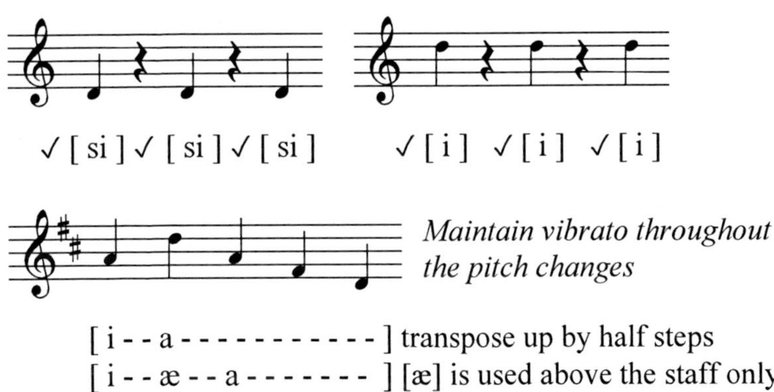

Maintain vibrato throughout the pitch changes

[i - - a - - - - - - - - - - -] transpose up by half steps
[i - - æ - - a - - - - - - -] [æ] is used above the staff only

Notes

Personal Assessment

Breath

Breath Control   70-------------79/80-------------89/90-------------100
Breath Expansion   70-------------79/80-------------89/90-------------100
Breath Support   70-------------79/80-------------89/90-------------100

Diction

Consonant Articulation   70-------------79/80-------------89/90-------------100
Vowel Formation   70-------------79/80-------------89/90-------------100

Musicianship

Expression   70-------------79/80-------------89/90-------------100
Legato   70-------------79/80-------------89/90-------------100
Pitch Accuracy   70-------------79/80-------------89/90-------------100
Rhythmic Accuracy   70-------------79/80-------------89/90-------------100

Posture and Tension

Postural Alignment   70-------------79/80-------------89/90-------------100
Release of Tension   70-------------79/80-------------89/90-------------100

Technique

Flexibility   70-------------79/80-------------89/90-------------100
Onset   70-------------79/80-------------89/90-------------100
Palatal Space   70-------------79/80-------------89/90-------------100
Pharyngeal Space   70-------------79/80-------------89/90-------------100
Projection   70-------------79/80-------------89/90-------------100
Vibrato   70-------------79/80-------------89/90-------------100
Tone Quality   70-------------79/80-------------89/90-------------100
Vowel Equalization   70-------------79/80-------------89/90-------------100

Equalizing the Scale

[ðɛ:ʌɾ ɪz no:ʊ sɛn'sɛ:ɪʃʌn ʌv 'ɹɛdʒɪstʌ ʧɛ:ɪndʒ ɪn ðʌ wɛl tɹɛ:ɪnd vɔ:ɪs]

[ʌ vɔ:ɪs ɪz 'ivɛn θɾu'a:ʊt ðʌ ɹɛ:ɪndʒ ʍɛn tɹɛ:ɪnd fɹʌm ðʌ tap da:ʊn]

[ɔl to:ʊnz ʃʊd bi sʌŋ ɪn 'ɹɛfɹɛns tu ði 'ʌpʌ ɹɛ:ɪndʒ]

[ʌb'zɜv ðʌ ɾɪ'lɛ:ɪʃʌnʃɪp ʌv ðʌ 'ha:ɹɛst tu 'lo:ʊɛst no:ʊt ɪn ðɪs 'sikwɛns]:

[ʌb'zɜv ðʌ 'ʧælɛndʒ ʌv 'sɪŋɪŋ ðʌ sɛ:ɪm to:ʊnz ɪn ʌ ɾɪ'vɜs da:ɪ'ɾɛkʃʌn]:

Connecting into the Top

[ði [u] fɔ'mɛ:ɪʃʌn pɹo'va:ɪdz æn 'ɛksɛlɛnt tul fɔ 'flɪpɪŋ 'ɪntu ðʌ tap]

['mɪmɪk ðʌ hɔn ʌv ʌ 'madʊl ɛ:ɪ fɔd [a'u:gʌ]]

['no:ʊtɪs ha:ʊ ðʌ vɔ:ɪs 'pɪvʌts 'izɪlɪ fɹʌm lo:ʊ tu ha:ɪ]?

[kʌ'nɛkt 'ɪntu ðʌ tap wɪð skɪps bɪ'fɔ:ɾ ʌ'tɛmptɪŋ ʌ'sɛndɪŋ skɛ:ɪlz]:

~Patricia McCaffrey

Application

['sɪŋ ðʌ tap no:ʊt ʌv ʌ fɹɛ:ɪz fɜst tu ɪ'stæblɪʃ æn 'ʌpʌ 'ɹɛfɹɛns pɔ:ɪnt]

Speaker's "ah" Formation

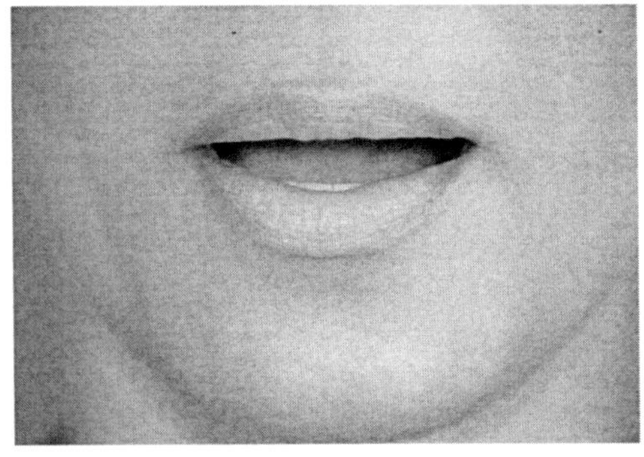

Singer's "ah" Formation

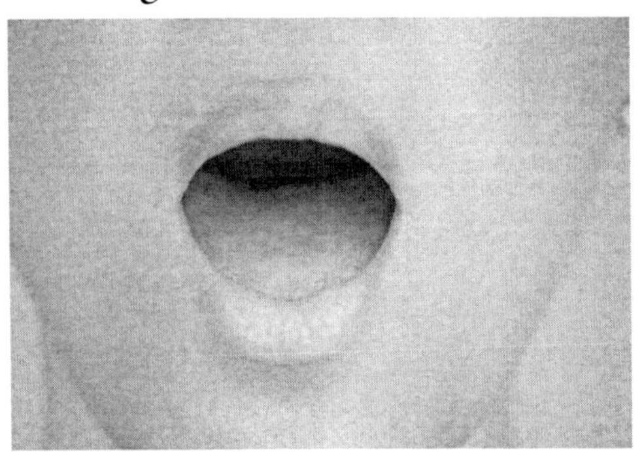

Singer's [æ] Formation

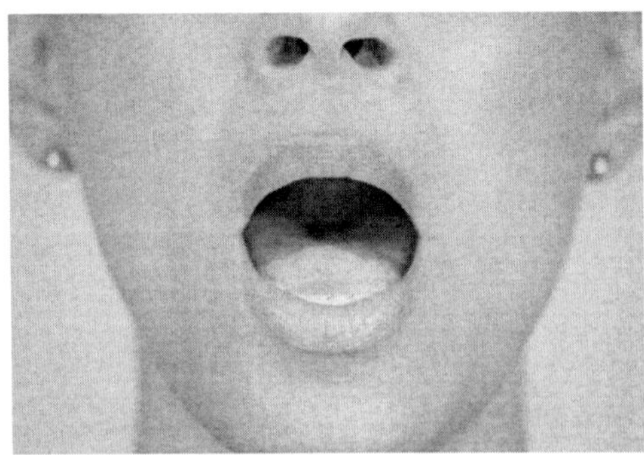

Exploring Palatal Resonance: Week 7

Day 1: Exploring Palatal Resonance – [ɑ]

Day 2: Exploring Palatal Resonance – [æ]

Day 3: Exploring Palatal Resonance – [a]

Day 4: Exploring Resonance

Day 5: Discovering Chiaroscuro

Day 6: Choral Singing vs Solo Singing

Lesson Notes, Date: _____________

Checklist of Concepts to Review

BREATH
Breath Control___
p: 35, 63, 67
Breath Support___
p: 63, 65
Breath Expansion___
p: 33, 35
DICTION
Articulation___
p: 121, 123, 125, 131
Front Vowels___
p: 57, 105
Back Vowels___
p: 73, 107
Central Vowels___
p: 89, 91, 93, 109, 111
Mixed Vowels___
p: 113, 115
FLEXIBILITY
Flexibility___
p: 109, 139
MUSICIANSHIP
Artistry___
p: 141
Dynamics___
p: 143
Legato___
p: 49, 59, 75, 139, 141

POSTURE
Postural Alignment___
p: 25, 27
RANGE
Range___
p: 81, 91, 139
TONE
Chiaroscuro___
p: 97, 113, 115
Lip Trills___
p: 41, 43
Palatal Resonance___
p: 89, 91, 93, 109
Pharyngeal Space___
p: 57, 59, 93, 105, 109
Projection___
p: 73, 75, 93, 107
Register___
p: 43, 83
Resonance___
p: 93, 95, 97, 109, 137
Sensory Awareness___
p: 61, 127
Vibrato___
p: 43, 45, 51, 77, 79, 81
Vowel Equalization___
p: 79, 95, 137
WARM-UPS___
p: 200-204

WARNINGS
Breathy Tone___
p: 35, 77, 113, 125, 127
Faulty Formation___
p. 111, 127
Faulty Movement___
p. 45, 47
Faulty Onset___
p: 59, 75, 127
Jaw Tension___
p: 31, 111, 121, 123, 125
Nasal Tone ___
p: 111, 127
Pressed Tone___
p: 35, 41, 43, 83
Spread Tone___
p: 57, 61, 73, 111
Tension___
p: 29, 31, 45, 47, 61
Tongue Impeded Tone__
p: 111, 127
OTHER
Choral Singing___
p: 99
Stage Deportment___
p: 145
Vocal health___
p: 147

Daily Notes and Practice Times

Day 1   Practice Time:___________

Day 2   Practice Time:___________

Day 3   Practice Time:___________

Day 4   Practice Time:___________

Day 5   Practice Time:___________

Day 6   Practice Time:___________

Notes

Personal Assessment

Breath

Breath Control	70--------------79/80--------------89/90--------------100
Breath Expansion	70--------------79/80--------------89/90--------------100
Breath Support	70--------------79/80--------------89/90--------------100

Diction

Consonant Articulation	70--------------79/80--------------89/90--------------100
Vowel Formation	70--------------79/80--------------89/90--------------100

Musicianship

Expression	70--------------79/80--------------89/90--------------100
Legato	70--------------79/80--------------89/90--------------100
Pitch Accuracy	70--------------79/80--------------89/90--------------100
Rhythmic Accuracy	70--------------79/80--------------89/90--------------100

Posture and Tension

Postural Alignment	70--------------79/80--------------89/90--------------100
Release of Tension	70--------------79/80--------------89/90--------------100

Technique

Flexibility	70--------------79/80--------------89/90--------------100
Onset	70--------------79/80--------------89/90--------------100
Palatal Space	70--------------79/80--------------89/90--------------100
Pharyngeal Space	70--------------79/80--------------89/90--------------100
Projection	70--------------79/80--------------89/90--------------100
Vibrato	70--------------79/80--------------89/90--------------100
Tone Quality	70--------------79/80--------------89/90--------------100
Vowel Equalization	70--------------79/80--------------89/90--------------100

Exploring Palatal Resonance – [ɑ]
(see image on page 84)

[ði [ɑ] fɔ spitʃ ɪz ˈmidɪʊl ɪn ˈplɛːɪsmɛnt ænd wɪðˈaːʊt ʌ ˈloːʊʌd dʒɔ]

[ði [ɑ] fɔ ˈsɪŋɪŋ hæz ʌ ɹɪˈlist dʒɔ ʍɪtʃ ɪkˈspændz ði ˈɔɾʊl ˈkævɪtɪ]:

  1.   [ðʌ saft ˈpælæt ɪz ɹɛːɪzd]

  2.   [ðʌ dʒɔ ɪz ɹɪˈlist]

  3.   [ðʌ tʌŋ laːɪz loːʊ an ðʌ flɔːʌɾ ʌv ðʌ maːʊθ]

  4.   [ðʌ tʌŋ tɪp ˈkantækts ðʌ ˈloːʊʌ fɹʌnt tiθ]

[ʌˈlaːʊ æt list tu ˈfɪŋgʌ wɪdθs spɛːɪs bɪˈtwin ðʌ ˈmoːʊlʌz]

[juz ʌ ˈmɪɾɔ tu ʌbˈzɜv ðʌ dʒɔ poˈzɪʃʌn]

[muv ðʌ dʒɔ fɹʌm saːɪd tu saːɪd tu ɹɪˈlis ˌɪntʌˈfɪːʌɾɪŋ ˈmʌskjulʌ ˈtɛnʃʌn]

Warnings

[du nat ʌˈlaːʊ ðʌ ˈɹɛzonæns ʌv dak [ɑ] tu fɔl loːʊ ɪn ðʌ θroːʊt]

[du nat spɹɛd ðʌ lɪps fɔ ðʌ fɔˈmɛːɪʃʌn ʌv [ɑ]]

[ʌˈvɔːɪd ʌ ˈglatʊl [ʔ] ɔ [h] ˈansɛt ʌv ðʌ toːʊn]

[ʌˈvɔːɪd ʌ ˈnɛːɪzʊl toːʊn (juz ˈpælæt lɪfts tu fil ðʌ ɹɪˈkwaːɪʌd spɛːɪs)]

Exercise: [kʌmˈbaːɪn lɪˈgatoːʊ wɪð vaːɹˈbɹatoːʊ tu ˈsɪŋ ðʌ ˈfaloːʊɪŋ]:

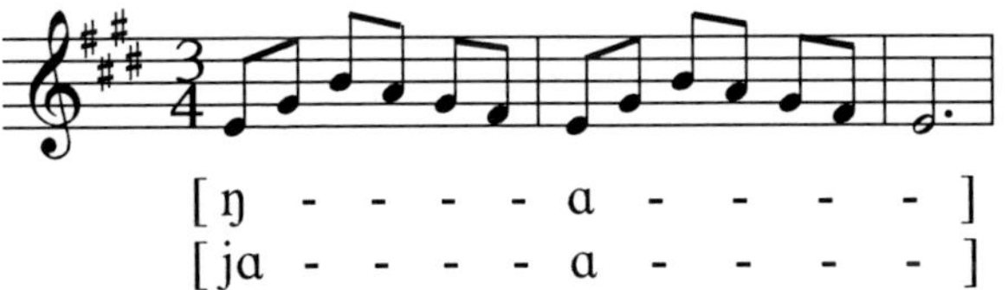

Notes

Personal Assessment

Breath
Breath Control   70-------------79/80-------------89/90-------------100
Breath Expansion   70-------------79/80-------------89/90-------------100
Breath Support   70-------------79/80-------------89/90-------------100

Diction
Consonant Articulation   70-------------79/80-------------89/90-------------100
Vowel Formation   70-------------79/80-------------89/90-------------100

Musicianship
Expression   70-------------79/80-------------89/90-------------100
Legato   70-------------79/80-------------89/90-------------100
Pitch Accuracy   70-------------79/80-------------89/90-------------100
Rhythmic Accuracy   70-------------79/80-------------89/90-------------100

Posture and Tension
Postural Alignment   70-------------79/80-------------89/90-------------100
Release of Tension   70-------------79/80-------------89/90-------------100

Technique
Flexibility   70-------------79/80-------------89/90-------------100
Onset   70-------------79/80-------------89/90-------------100
Palatal Space   70-------------79/80-------------89/90-------------100
Pharyngeal Space   70-------------79/80-------------89/90-------------100
Projection   70-------------79/80-------------89/90-------------100
Vibrato   70-------------79/80-------------89/90-------------100
Tone Quality   70-------------79/80-------------89/90-------------100
Vowel Equalization   70-------------79/80-------------89/90-------------100

Exploring Palatal Resonance – [æ]

[ði [æ] vaːʊʌl ɪz pɜˈsivd æz æn ˌʌndɪˈzaːɪʌɾʌbʊl saːʊnd fɔ ˈsɪŋɪŋ]

[ði [æ] saːʊnd ɪz ʌ kæɾæktʌˈɾɪstɪk ʌv ði ˈɪŋglɪʃ ˈlæŋgwæʤ]

[ɪts fɔˈmeːɪʃʌn pɹoˈvaːɪdz ʌ ˈvæljuʌbʊl ʃeːɪp fɔ dɪsˈkʌvʌɾɪŋ ˈʌpʌ toːʊnz]

Tongue Push-Ups

[tʌŋ aʧ ˈɛksʌsaːɪzɛz ɹɪˈpɹoːʊgɹæm ðʌ spiʧ ˈmʌsʊlz fɔ ˈsɪŋɪŋ]

1. [ɹɪˈlis ðʌ ʤɔ fɔ [a] ænd ɹeːɪz ðʌ saft ˈpælæt]

2. [ðʌ tʌŋ laːɪz loːʊ ænd flæt an ðʌ flɔːɾ ʌv ðʌ maːʊθ]

3. [ðʌ tʌŋ tɪp ˈkantækts ðʌ ˈloːʊʌ fɹʌnt tiθ fɔ ði ɪnˈtaːɪʌ ˈɛksʌsaːɪz]

4. [ðʌ lɪps a ˈnaːɪðʌ ˈɹaːʊndɛd nɔ spɹɛd]

5. [fɔm [æ] baːɪ ˈaʧɪŋ ðʌ tʌŋ ʌ ˈlɪtʊl ˈfɔwʊd (ʧɛk ɪn ʌ ˈmɪɾɔ)]

6. [du nat spɹɛd ðʌ lɪps nɔ ˈɔltʌ ðʌ poˈzɪʃʌn ʌv ðʌ ʤɔ]

7. [ˈɔltʌˌneːɪt bɪˈtwin [a] ænd [æ] baːɪ minz ʌv tʌŋ ˈmuvmɛnt ˈoːʊnlɪ]

8. [meːɪnˈteːɪn ði [a] lɪp ænd ʤɔ poˈzɪʃʌn]

Warnings

[ði [æ] ˈvaːʊʌl meːɪ saːʊnd ʃɹɪl tu ðʌ ˈsɪŋʌz iːʌ]

[du nat ʌˈʤʌst ɪts fɔˈmeːɪʃʌn beːɪst an ði iːʌz ʌˈsɛsmɛnt ʌv ðʌ ˈvaːʊʌl]

The sensation of vibrancy should guide the singer to an accurate formation and optimal resonance of [æ].

Notes

The formations of vowels are indicated below:

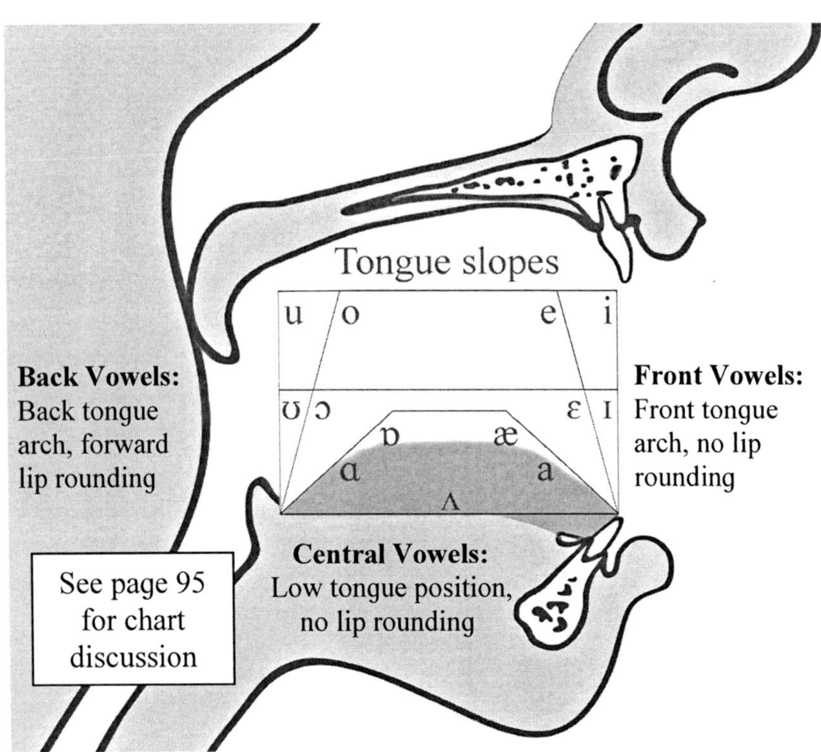

Exploring Palatal Resonance – [a]

[bɹɑːɪt [a] ɪz ði ɪˈtæljæn "ah" ˈvɑːʊʌl fɔmd wɪð ʌ ɹɪˈlist dʒɔ]

Its formation is similar to dark [ɑ] with the added feel of a smile in the upper cheeks, palate, and eyes. Bright [a] compels the singer to focus the tone without reliance on tongue arch or lip rounding.

[θɪŋk bɹɑːɪt ɑːɪz ʌɛn ˈsɪŋɪŋ ði [a] ˈvɑːʊʌl]

[bɹɑːɪt [a] ɪz ˈɔlsoːʊ fɑːʊnd ɪn ðʌ ˈdʒɜmæn ænd fɹɛntʃ ˈlæŋgwædʒɛz]

Bright [a] (voilà), back [ɒ] (hot), and front [e] (ch<u>ao</u>s) are not included in English lyric transcription. A bright [a] sound is between [æ] and [ɑ]; [ɒ] is between [ɑ] and [ɔ]; and [e] is between [i] and [ɛ].

[ðʌ fɔˈmɛːɪʃʌnz ʌv ˈvɑːʊʌlz ɑ ˈɪndɪkɛːɪtɪd ɑn pɛːɪdʒ 92]

Tongue Arch
The pitch (angle) of the tongue arch is provided here:

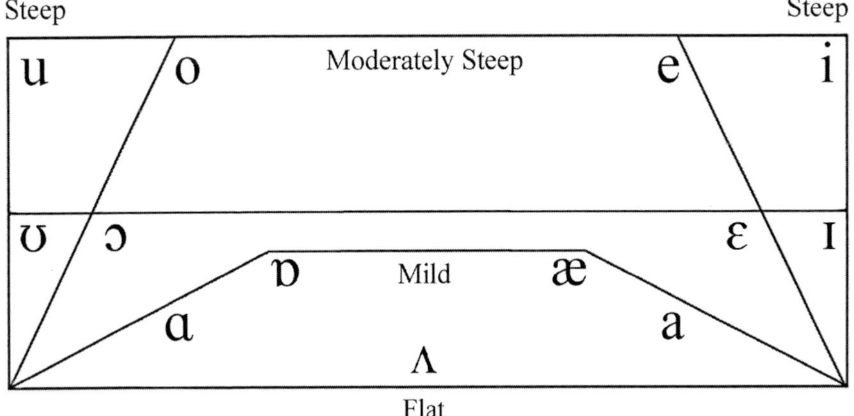

Back vowels are to the left of the chart, front vowels are to the right, central vowels are in the center, closed vowels are in the upper section, open vowels are in the lower section.

Consider the direction of your air flow once it leaves your mouth. Does it angle up, down, or straight ahead? Which is optimal?

Notes

Personal Assessment

Breath
Breath Control   70-------------79/80-------------89/90-------------100
Breath Expansion   70-------------79/80-------------89/90-------------100
Breath Support   70-------------79/80-------------89/90-------------100

Diction
Consonant Articulation 70-------------79/80-------------89/90-------------100
Vowel Formation   70-------------79/80-------------89/90-------------100

Musicianship
Expression   70-------------79/80-------------89/90-------------100
Legato   70-------------79/80-------------89/90-------------100
Pitch Accuracy   70-------------79/80-------------89/90-------------100
Rhythmic Accuracy   70-------------79/80-------------89/90-------------100

Posture and Tension
Postural Alignment   70-------------79/80-------------89/90-------------100
Release of Tension   70-------------79/80-------------89/90-------------100

Technique
Flexibility   70-------------79/80-------------89/90-------------100
Onset   70-------------79/80-------------89/90-------------100
Palatal Space   70-------------79/80-------------89/90-------------100
Pharyngeal Space   70-------------79/80-------------89/90-------------100
Projection   70-------------79/80-------------89/90-------------100
Vibrato   70-------------79/80-------------89/90-------------100
Tone Quality   70-------------79/80-------------89/90-------------100
Vowel Equalization   70-------------79/80-------------89/90-------------100

Exploring Resonance
(See chart on page 92)

[θɾi ˈfæktɔz dɪˈtɜmɪn ˈɹezonæns – ʃɛːɪp ɔɾɪenˈtɛːɪʃʌn ænd ˈmuvmɛnt]

[foˈnɛtɪklɪ ˈspikɪŋ ðiz tɜmz mɛːɪ bi dɪˈfaːɪnd æz]:

1. [pɔːɪnt ʌv aˈtɪkjulɛːɪʃʌn (ʃɛːɪp fɔmd baːɪ ðʌ tʌŋ ɔ lɪp poˈzɪʃʌn)]

2. [ˈmænʌɾ ʌv aˈtɪkjulɛːɪʃʌn (ɔɾɪenˈtɛːɪʃʌn ʌv ði ɛːʌ floːʊ/vaːɪˈbɹatoːʊ)]

3. [ˈvɔːɪsɪŋ (ɪnˈgɛːɪdʒɪŋ ðʌ vɔːɪs ʍaːɪl ˈmuvɪŋ ði ɛːʌ)]

Observing point and manner of articulation helps a singer discover the boundaries of a vowel shape, explore the location of resonance, and anticipate the movement of vocalized air flow.

[ˈsɛntɹʊl "ah" pɹoˈvaːɪdz ðʌ fʌndʌˈmɛntʊl spɛːɪs fɔɾ ɔl ˈvaːʊʌlz]

[dɪsˈkʌvʌɾɪŋ ʌ ˈɹezonænt toːʊn ɪz ɹɪˈlaːɪænt an ˈaptɪmaːɪzɪŋ "ah"]

[ðɪs ɪz ʌˈkamplɪʃt θɾu ˈvaːʊʌl ɛksploˈɾɛːɪʃʌn]

Front vowels increase pharyngeal space (the bulk of the tongue is forward), back vowels focus and project the tone (the lips are rounded and forward), and central vowels expand the oral cavity (space is not limited by tongue or lip formation). All vowels hook into the same resonant core once "ah" is optimized.

[lɪst ðʌ θɾi ˈɪŋglɪʃ fɹʌnt ˈvaːʊʌlz]:

[lɪst ðʌ fɔːʌ ˈɪŋglɪʃ bæk ˈvaːʊʌlz]:

[lɪst ðʌ fɔːʌ ˈɪŋglɪʃ ˈsɛntɹʊl ˈvaːʊʌlz]:

Notes

Personal Assessment

Breath

Breath Control	70-------------79/80-------------89/90-------------100
Breath Expansion	70-------------79/80-------------89/90-------------100
Breath Support	70-------------79/80-------------89/90-------------100

Diction

Consonant Articulation	70-------------79/80-------------89/90-------------100
Vowel Formation	70-------------79/80-------------89/90-------------100

Musicianship

Expression	70-------------79/80-------------89/90-------------100
Legato	70-------------79/80-------------89/90-------------100
Pitch Accuracy	70-------------79/80-------------89/90-------------100
Rhythmic Accuracy	70-------------79/80-------------89/90-------------100

Posture and Tension

Postural Alignment	70-------------79/80-------------89/90-------------100
Release of Tension	70-------------79/80-------------89/90-------------100

Technique

Flexibility	70-------------79/80-------------89/90-------------100
Onset	70-------------79/80-------------89/90-------------100
Palatal Space	70-------------79/80-------------89/90-------------100
Pharyngeal Space	70-------------79/80-------------89/90-------------100
Projection	70-------------79/80-------------89/90-------------100
Vibrato	70-------------79/80-------------89/90-------------100
Tone Quality	70-------------79/80-------------89/90-------------100
Vowel Equalization	70-------------79/80-------------89/90-------------100

Discovering Chiaroscuro

[ˈkjaɾoskuɾo ɪz æn ɪˈtæljæn bɛl ˈkanto tɜm ˈminɪŋ bɹaːɪt/dak]

[ɪʧ ˈvaːʊʌl hæz ʌ dɪsˈtɪŋktɪv ˈkʌlɔɾ ɔ kæræktʌˈɾɪstɪk]

[fɹʌnt ˈvaːʊʌlz hæv ʌ ˈbɹɪljænt ˈkwalɪtɪ (ˈkjaɾo)]

[bæk ˈvaːʊʌlz hæv ʌ dak ɹɪʧ ˈkwalɪtɪ (ˈskuɾo)]

[ˈmɪksɪŋ ˈvaːʊʌl ˈkwalɪtɪz ʌˈlaːʊz ðʌ ˈsɪŋʌ tu dɪsˈkʌvʌ ˈkjaɾoskuɾo]

The Uniqueness of Each Voice

[ˈɹɛzonænt spɛːɪs/toːʊn ˈkwalɪtɪ ɪz æz juˈnik æz ðʌ ˈsɪŋʌz ˈfɪŋɡʌ pɹɪnt]

[wʌn vɔːɪs mɛːɪ ˈfɛːɪvɔɾ æn [a] spɛːɪs ʍaːɪl ʌˈnʌðʌ ˈfɛːɪvɔz æn [i] spɛːɪs]

[ˈvaːʊʌl ˈmɪksɪŋ ˈɔlsoːʊ ʌˈlaːʊz ðʌ ˈsɪŋʌ tu ˈaptɪmaːɪz ˈvaːɪbɹænsɪ]

These adjustments may be considered only after formation of the primary vowels is clearly established.

[ˈɹɛzonæns ʌv [i] mɛːɪ bi ˈbaɾoːʊd ɪf ʌ toːʊn ɪz tu ˈhɛvɪ ɔ dak]

[ðɪs ɪz ʌˈkamplɪʃt baːɪ ˈsɪŋɪŋ wɪð æn [i] tʌŋ ɪn ði [a] spɛːɪs]

[ˈɹɛzonæns ʌv [ɔ] mɛːɪ bi ˈbaɾoːʊd ɪf ʌ toːʊn ɪz θɪn ɔ ʃɹɪl]

[ðɪs ɪz ʌˈkamplɪʃt baːɪ ˈsɪŋɪŋ æn [a] ˈvaːʊʌl wɪð [ɔ] lɪp ˈɹaːʊndɪŋ]

[ðʌ ˈsɪŋʌz ɪːʌ kæˈnat bi ˈtɹʌstɛd tu mɛːɪk ðɪz dɪtɜmɪnˈɛːɪʃʌnz]

The singer's ear creates an internal perception of the vowel which is misleading. For example, the "ah" can have up to 5 sounds in the singer's ear. It may sound like an [ɑ], [a], [ʌ], [ɔ], or even [æ] sound.

Notes

Personal Assessment

Breath
Breath Control   70-------------79/80-------------89/90-------------100
Breath Expansion   70-------------79/80-------------89/90-------------100
Breath Support   70-------------79/80-------------89/90-------------100

Diction
Consonant Articulation 70-------------79/80-------------89/90-------------100
Vowel Formation   70-------------79/80-------------89/90-------------100

Musicianship
Expression   70-------------79/80-------------89/90-------------100
Legato   70-------------79/80-------------89/90-------------100
Pitch Accuracy   70-------------79/80-------------89/90-------------100
Rhythmic Accuracy   70-------------79/80-------------89/90-------------100

Posture and Tension
Postural Alignment   70-------------79/80-------------89/90-------------100
Release of Tension   70-------------79/80-------------89/90-------------100

Technique
Flexibility   70-------------79/80-------------89/90-------------100
Onset   70-------------79/80-------------89/90-------------100
Palatal Space   70-------------79/80-------------89/90-------------100
Pharyngeal Space   70-------------79/80-------------89/90-------------100
Projection   70-------------79/80-------------89/90-------------100
Vibrato   70-------------79/80-------------89/90-------------100
Tone Quality   70-------------79/80-------------89/90-------------100
Vowel Equalization   70-------------79/80-------------89/90-------------100

Choral Singing vs Solo Singing

[ˈmɛnɪ ˈsɪŋʌz dɪsˈkʌvʌ ðɛːʌ lʌv fɔ ˈsɪŋɪŋ ʍaːɪl ɪn ˈkwaːɪʌ]

[ʌ ˈkɔɾʊl ˈbækgɹaːʊnd pɹoˈvaːɪdz ʌ ˈkɔɾʊl ˈdɪkʃʌn fɹɛːɪm ʌv ˈɹɛfɹɛns]

[ˈkɔɾʊl ˈvaːʊʌlz ænd ˈkansonænts aɾ ɪˈstæblɪʃt tu ˈjunɪˌfaːɪ ðʌ gɾup]

[ðʌ ˈsoːʊloɪsts ˈvaːʊʌlz aɾ ɪˈstæblɪʃt tu ˈbjutɪfaːɪ ænd pɹoˈdʒɛkt wʌn vɔːɪs]

[sʌm ˈvaːʊʌlz ([i] ɪn paˈtɪkjulʌ) a tu haʃ ʍɛn ˈæmplɪfaːɪd an mæs]

Warnings

Choral singing is a careful coordination of many voices articulating in a unified manner. Each member of the group becomes acutely aware of supporting a singular articulation, especially for final "s". For many singers, this is interpreted into a weakening of the vowel. Some have established the habit of covering the vowel sound or diminishing the vibrato in order to blend with the group. Consonants may be weakened as well.

Solution

[ʌndʌˈstænd ðæt ˈkɔɾʊl ænd ˈsoːʊloːʊ ˈvɔːɪsez hæv juˈnik ˈfʌŋkʃʌnz]

[ðʌ ˈkɔɾʊl ˈsɪŋʌ mʌst bi ˈsɛnsɪtɪv tu ðʌ blɛnd ʌv ðʌ gɾup]

[ðʌ ˈsoːʊloːʊ ˈsɪŋʌɾ ɪz ˈsoːʊli ɾɪˈspansɪbʊl fɔ]:

1. [ˈvaːɪbɹænsɪ ʌv ðʌ toːʊn (vaːɪˈbɹatoːʊ)]

2. [ˈklæɾɪtɪ ʌv ðʌ ˈvaːʊʌl (ˈvaːʊʌl fɔˈmɛːɪʃʌn)]

3. [pɹoˈdʒɛkʃʌn ʌv ðʌ tɛkst (ˈkansonænt aˈtɪkjulɛːɪʃʌn)]

Vowel Chart

Front	Back	Mixed	Central
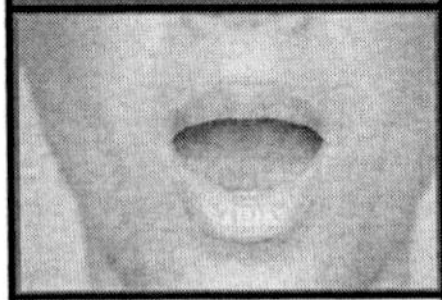	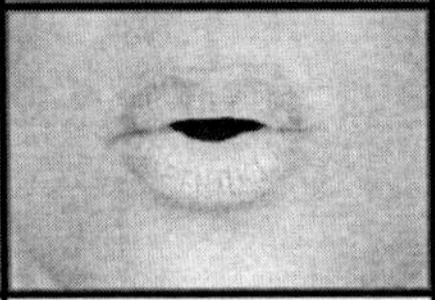	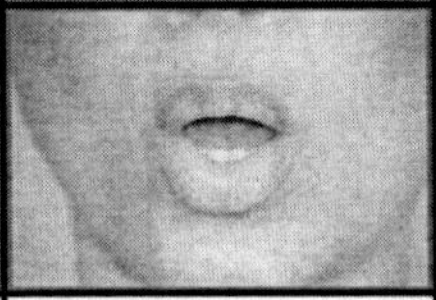	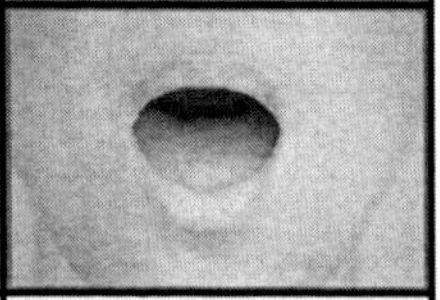
[i]	[u]	[y]	[æ]
[ɪ]	[ʊ]	[ʏ]	[a]
[e]	[o]	[ø]	[ɑ]
[ɛ]	[ɔ]	[œ]	[ʌ]

Vowel modification alters the shape of a vowel to expand the space. Vowel migration maintains the formation of the *closed* vowels (in the "ah" space) to maximize the focus and space of *open* vowels. Vowel terms are defined on page 152.

Exploring the Secondary Vowels: Week 8

Day 1: Exploring Pharyngeal Space –
Front Vowels

Day 2: Exploring Projection –
Back Vowels

Day 3: Exploring Palatal Resonance – [ʌ]

Day 4: Optimizing [ɜ]

Day 5: Exploring Chiaroscuro – [y] and [ʏ]

Day 6: Exploring Chiaroscuro – [ø] and [œ]

Lesson Notes, Date: _________

Checklist of Concepts to Review

BREATH
Breath Control___
p: 35, 63, 67
Breath Support___
p: 63, 65
Breath Expansion___
p: 33, 35
DICTION
Articulation___
p: 121, 123, 125, 131
Front Vowels___
p: 57, 105
Back Vowels___
p: 73, 107
Central Vowels___
p: 89, 91, 93, 109, 111
Mixed Vowels___
p: 113, 115
FLEXIBILITY
Flexibility___
p: 109, 139
MUSICIANSHIP
Artistry___
p: 141
Dynamics___
p: 143
Legato___
p: 49, 59, 75, 139, 141

POSTURE
Postural Alignment___
p: 25, 27
RANGE
Range___
p: 81, 91, 139
TONE
Chiaroscuro___
p: 97, 113, 115
Lip Trills___
p: 41, 43
Palatal Resonance___
p: 89, 91, 93, 109
Pharyngeal Space___
p: 57, 59, 93, 105, 109
Projection___
p: 73, 75, 93, 107
Register___
p: 43, 83
Resonance___
p: 93, 95, 97, 109, 137
Sensory Awareness___
p: 61, 127
Vibrato___
p: 43, 45, 51, 77, 79, 81
Vowel Equalization___
p: 79, 95, 137
WARM-UPS___
p: 200-204

WARNINGS
Breathy Tone___
p: 35, 77, 113, 125, 127
Faulty Formation___
p. 111, 127
Faulty Movement___
p. 45, 47
Faulty Onset___
p: 59, 75, 127
Jaw Tension___
p: 31, 111, 121, 123, 125
Nasal Tone___
p: 111, 127
Pressed Tone___
p: 35, 41, 43, 83
Spread Tone___
p: 57, 61, 73, 111
Tension___
p: 29, 31, 45, 47, 61
Tongue Impeded Tone__
p: 111, 127
OTHER
Choral Singing___
p: 99
Stage Deportment___
p: 145
Vocal health___
p: 147

Daily Notes and Practice Times

Day 1   Practice Time:__________

Day 2   Practice Time:__________

Day 3   Practice Time:__________

Day 4   Practice Time:__________

Day 5   Practice Time:__________

Day 6   Practice Time:__________

Notes

Personal Assessment

Breath

Breath Control   70-------------79/80-------------89/90-------------100
Breath Expansion   70-------------79/80-------------89/90-------------100
Breath Support   70-------------79/80-------------89/90-------------100

Diction

Consonant Articulation 70-------------79/80-------------89/90-------------100
Vowel Formation   70-------------79/80-------------89/90-------------100

Musicianship

Expression   70-------------79/80-------------89/90-------------100
Legato   70-------------79/80-------------89/90-------------100
Pitch Accuracy   70-------------79/80-------------89/90-------------100
Rhythmic Accuracy   70-------------79/80-------------89/90-------------100

Posture and Tension

Postural Alignment   70-------------79/80-------------89/90-------------100
Release of Tension   70-------------79/80-------------89/90-------------100

Technique

Flexibility   70-------------79/80-------------89/90-------------100
Onset   70-------------79/80-------------89/90-------------100
Palatal Space   70-------------79/80-------------89/90-------------100
Pharyngeal Space   70-------------79/80-------------89/90-------------100
Projection   70-------------79/80-------------89/90-------------100
Vibrato   70-------------79/80-------------89/90-------------100
Tone Quality   70-------------79/80-------------89/90-------------100
Vowel Equalization   70-------------79/80-------------89/90-------------100

Exploring Pharyngeal Space – Front Vowels

[kloːʊzd [i] hæz ðʌ moːʊst ˈfɔwʊd tʌŋ aʧ]

[kloːʊzd [u] hæz ðʌ moːʊst ˈfɔwʊd lɪp ˈɹaːʊndɪŋ]

[ˈsɛntɹʊl [ʌ] ˈaptɪmaːɪzez spɛːɪs wɪðˈaːʊt tʌŋ ˈfɹʌntɪŋ ɔ lɪp ˈɹaːʊndɪŋ]

[ðiz θɾi ˈvaːʊʌlz a ðʌ ˈpɹaːɪmɛɾɪ ˈvaːʊʌlz]

[ɔl ˈʌðʌ ˈvaːʊʌlz a dɪˈɾɪvʌtɪvz ʌv ðiz fɔˈmɛːɪʃʌnz]

[dɪˈɾɪvʌtɪv ˈvaːʊʌlz a ðʌ ˈsɛkʌndɛɾɪ ˈvaːʊʌlz]

[ˈmastʌɾɪ ʌv kloːʊzd [i] pɹɪˈpɛːʌz ðʌ sɪŋʌ fɔ ˈsɛkʌndɛɾɪ fɹʌnt ˈvaːʊʌlz]

[ði ˈæŋgʊl ʌv ðʌ tʌŋ aʧ ɪz ˈsɪmɪlʌ fɔɾ ɔl fɹʌnt ˈvaːʊʌlz]

[fɔm [e] [ɪ] ænd [ɛ] wɪð spɛːɪs ʌv [a] ænd ʌ fa ˈfɔwʊd tʌŋ aʧ]

[ðɪs ʌˈpɹoːʊʧ ˈmæksɪmaːɪzez ðʌ fʌˈɾɪndʒʊl spɛːɪs]

[ði ˈɔdʌɾ ʌv ˈvaːʊʌlz fɹʌm kloːʊzd tu ˈoːʊpɛn ɪz æz ˈfaloːʊz]:

      Closed [i] [e] to [ɪ] [ɛ] Open

[juz ðʌ tʌŋ pʊʃ ʌps ˈɛksʌsaːɪz tu ɪkˈsplɔːɾ ɔl fɹʌnt ˈvaːʊʌlz]

[mɛːɪnˈtɛːɪn ðʌ spɛːɪs ʌv [a] ʍaːɪl ɪnˈtoːʊnɪŋ ðʌ ˈfaloːʊɪŋ ˈsikwɛns]:

      Tongue push-ups: [a] [i] [a] [e] [a] [ɪ] [a] [ɛ] [a]

Reminder: [ˈsɪŋɪŋ stats wɪð spɛːɪs] *Singing is: space, support, spin.*

[ˈvaːʊʌl fɔˈmɛːɪʃʌn ˈfaloːʊz bʌt ˈnɛvʌɾ æt ði ɪkˈspɛns ʌv spɛːɪs]

Notes

Personal Assessment

Breath

Breath Control   70--------------79/80-------------89/90-------------100
Breath Expansion   70--------------79/80-------------89/90-------------100
Breath Support   70--------------79/80-------------89/90-------------100

Diction

Consonant Articulation 70--------------79/80-------------89/90-------------100
Vowel Formation   70--------------79/80-------------89/90-------------100

Musicianship

Expression   70--------------79/80-------------89/90-------------100
Legato   70--------------79/80-------------89/90-------------100
Pitch Accuracy   70--------------79/80-------------89/90-------------100
Rhythmic Accuracy   70--------------79/80-------------89/90-------------100

Posture and Tension

Postural Alignment   70--------------79/80-------------89/90-------------100
Release of Tension   70--------------79/80-------------89/90-------------100

Technique

Flexibility   70--------------79/80-------------89/90-------------100
Onset   70--------------79/80-------------89/90-------------100
Palatal Space   70--------------79/80-------------89/90-------------100
Pharyngeal Space   70--------------79/80-------------89/90-------------100
Projection   70--------------79/80-------------89/90-------------100
Vibrato   70--------------79/80-------------89/90-------------100
Tone Quality   70--------------79/80-------------89/90-------------100
Vowel Equalization   70--------------79/80-------------89/90-------------100

Exploring Projection – Back Vowels

[ðʌ toːʊnz a ɾɪˈlist ʍɛn ðʌ ˈkansɛpt ʌv pɹoˈdʒɛkʃʌn ɪz ʌˈplaːɪd]

[bæk ˈvaːʊʌlz hæv ˈfɔwʊd lɪp ˈɹaːʊndɪŋ ɪnˈɪʃiɛːɪtɛd baːɪ ðʌ ʧik ˈmʌsʊlz]

[pɹoˈdʒɛkʃʌn ɪz ɪnˈhanst baːɪ ði ɪnˈtɛnʃʌnʊl ˈfɔwʊd ˈɹaːʊndɪŋ ʌv ðʌ lɪps]

[ˈmastʌɾɪ ʌv kloːʊzd [u] pɹɪˈpɛːʌz ðʌ sɪŋʌ fɔ ˈsɛkʌndɛɾɪ bæk ˈvaːʊʌlz]

[ðʌ ˈɹaːʊndɛd pɹoˈdʒɛkʃʌn ʌv ðʌ lɪpz ɪz ˈsɪmɪlʌ fɔr ɔl bæk ˈvaːʊʌlz]

[fɔm [o] [ʊ] ænd [ɔ] wɪð ðʌ spɛːɪs ʌv [a] ænd ˈfɔwʊd ˈɹaːʊndɪŋ]

[ðɪs ʌˈpɹoːʊʧ ˈmæksɪmaːɪzɛz ðʌ pɹoˈdʒɛkʃʌn ʌv ðʌ toːʊn]

[ði ˈɔdʌɾ ʌv ˈvaːʊʌlz fɹʌm kloːʊzd tu ˈoːʊpɛn ɪz æz ˈfaloːʊz]:

     Closed [u] [o] to [ʊ] [ɔ] Open

[juz ðʌ lɪp ˈɹaːʊndɪŋ ˈɛksʌsaːɪz tu ɪkˈsploːʌɾ ɔl bæk ˈvaːʊʌlz]

[mɛːɪnˈtɛːɪn ðʌ spɛːɪs ʌv [a] ʍaːɪl ɪnˈtoːʊnɪŋ ðʌ ˈfaloːʊɪŋ ˈsikwɛns]:

     Lip rounds: [a] [u] [a] [o] [a] [ʊ] [a] [ɔ] [a]

[kloːʊzd ˈvaːʊʌlz mɛːɪ faːɪnd ʌ ˈfɔltɪ ˈɹɛzonæns ɪn ðʌ ˈnɛːɪzʊl ˈkævɪtɪz]

Remedy: [sɪŋ ðʌ ˈvaːʊʌl wɪð ˈklæɾɪtɪ ænd ˈɹæpɪdlɪ aˈtɪkjulɛːɪt ðʌ [n]]:

~ George Bitzas

Notes

Personal Assessment

Breath
Breath Control   70-------------79/80-------------89/90-------------100
Breath Expansion   70-------------79/80-------------89/90-------------100
Breath Support   70-------------79/80-------------89/90-------------100

Diction
Consonant Articulation 70-------------79/80-------------89/90-------------100
Vowel Formation   70-------------79/80-------------89/90-------------100

Musicianship
Expression   70-------------79/80-------------89/90-------------100
Legato   70-------------79/80-------------89/90-------------100
Pitch Accuracy   70-------------79/80-------------89/90-------------100
Rhythmic Accuracy   70-------------79/80-------------89/90-------------100

Posture and Tension
Postural Alignment 70-------------79/80-------------89/90-------------100
Release of Tension 70-------------79/80-------------89/90-------------100

Technique
Flexibility   70-------------79/80-------------89/90-------------100
Onset   70-------------79/80-------------89/90-------------100
Palatal Space   70-------------79/80-------------89/90-------------100
Pharyngeal Space   70-------------79/80-------------89/90-------------100
Projection   70-------------79/80-------------89/90-------------100
Vibrato   70-------------79/80-------------89/90-------------100
Tone Quality   70-------------79/80-------------89/90-------------100
Vowel Equalization 70-------------79/80-------------89/90-------------100

Exploring Palatal Resonance – [ʌ]

[ˈspoːʊkɛn ˈɪŋglɪʃ ɪz ˈtɪpɪklɪ ˈmidɪʊl ɪn ˈplɛːɪsmɛnt ([ʌ] ɪn paˈtɪkjulʌ)]

[ðʌ ˈsɛntɹʊl [ʌ] ˈvaːʊʌl ɪz ðʌ stɔl ˈvaːʊʌl (ði "uh" saːʊnd) ɪn ˈɪŋglɪʃ]

[ði [ʌ] fɔ ˈsɪŋɪŋ mʌst hæv jɔn spɛːɪs ænd ˈpælætʊl ˈɹɛzonæns]

Imagery: The 13-Story Building

[ˈɹɛzonænt spɛːɪs kæn bi kʌmˈpɛːʌd tu ðʌ flɔz ʌv ʌ ˈθɜtin ˈstɔɹɪ ˈbɪldɪŋ]

[ðʌ ˈθɜtinθ flɔːʌ ˈhaːʊzɛz ðʌ ˈnɛːɪzʊl ˈkævɪtɪz]

[ɪt ɪz æn ˈɪntɹɛstɪŋ plɛːɪs tu ɪkˈsplɔːʌ bʌt ju doːʊnt want tu lɪv ðɛːʌ]

[ðʌ twɛlfθ flɔːʌ hæz ʌ tɔl ˈsilɪŋ wɪð ˈwʊdɛn flɔːʌz ænd ˈmabʊl wɔlz]

[flɔːʌz wʌn θɹu ɪˈlɛvɛn hæv ˈmɛnɪ ɹɹumz bʌt ɔl a af ˈlɪmɪts]

[ðɛːɪ a ˈdɛːɪndʒʌɹʌslɪ kloːʊs tu ðʌ ˈmɛkænɪzʌm ʌv ðʌ ˈglatʊl stap]

[ðʌ twɛlfθ flɔːʌɹ ɪz ˈaptɪmʊl wɪð ɪts spɛːɪs ʃɛːɪp ænd ˈtɛksʧʊ]

[ˈaptɪmʊl ˈɹɛzonæns ɹɪˈzaːɪdz ɪn ðʌ haːɪt ʌv ðʌ ʃʌˈɹɪndʒʊl/ˈpælætʊl spɛːɪs]

Exercise

[ðʌ ˈsɛntɹʊl [ʌ] ˈvaːʊʌl ɪz æn ˈɛksɛlɛnt tul fɔ ˈmuvɪŋ ðʌ vɔːɪs]

[sɪŋ ðʌ ˈfaloːʊɪŋ ˈɛksʌsaːɪz ɪn ðʌ loːʊʌ ɹɛːɪndʒ æt ʌ ˈɹæpɪd ˈtempoːʊ]:

Notes

Personal Assessment

Breath
Breath Control   70-------------79/80-------------89/90-------------100
Breath Expansion   70-------------79/80-------------89/90-------------100
Breath Support   70-------------79/80-------------89/90-------------100

Diction
Consonant Articulation 70-------------79/80-------------89/90-------------100
Vowel Formation   70-------------79/80-------------89/90-------------100

Musicianship
Expression   70-------------79/80-------------89/90-------------100
Legato   70-------------79/80-------------89/90-------------100
Pitch Accuracy   70-------------79/80-------------89/90-------------100
Rhythmic Accuracy   70-------------79/80-------------89/90-------------100

Posture and Tension
Postural Alignment   70-------------79/80-------------89/90-------------100
Release of Tension   70-------------79/80-------------89/90-------------100

Technique
Flexibility   70-------------79/80-------------89/90-------------100
Onset   70-------------79/80-------------89/90-------------100
Palatal Space   70-------------79/80-------------89/90-------------100
Pharyngeal Space   70-------------79/80-------------89/90-------------100
Projection   70-------------79/80-------------89/90-------------100
Vibrato   70-------------79/80-------------89/90-------------100
Tone Quality   70-------------79/80-------------89/90-------------100
Vowel Equalization   70-------------79/80-------------89/90-------------100

Optimizing [з]

[ði [з] ˈvaːʊʌl ɪz ði ˈoːʊnlɪ ˈvaːʊʌl fɔmd wɪð ʌ ˈɹɛtɹoːʊflɛks tʌŋ]

[æn ˈʌpwʊd kɜld tʌŋ ɪz æn ˌʌndɪˈzaːɪʌɾʌbʊl fɔˈmɛːɪʃʌn fɔ ˈsɪŋɪŋ]

[ðɪs tʌŋ poˈzɪʃʌn ɪmˈpidz ði ɛːʌ floːʊ]

[ði [з] fɔˈmɛːɪʃʌn kæn bi ˈɔltʌd ɪf ˈnɛsɪsɛɹɪ (*si noːʊt bɪˈloːʊ)]

[ˈnoːʊtɪs ðʌ tʌŋ aʧ ɪn ðʌ bæk ʌv ðʌ maːʊθ wɪð ði [з] fɔˈmɛːɪʃʌn]

[mɛːɪnˈtɛːɪn ði aʧ ˈloːʊʌ ðʌ tʌŋ tɪp ænd ɹɪˈpit ðʌ fɹɛːɪz]:

"This is the sound of a tongue-impeded tone."

[ˈsɪŋɪŋ wɪð ʌ bæk aʧ ˈɹɛplɪkɛːɪts ðʌ vɔːɪs ʌv ˈkɜmɪt ðʌ fɹag]

[ʌ ˈsɪŋʌ mɛːɪ dɪˈsaːɪd ðɪs poˈzɪʃʌn filz sɛːɪf ænd ˈfoːʊkʌst]

[ðæt ɪz ʌ flɔd pɜˈsɛpʃʌn sɪns ðʌ toːʊn ɪz ˈfoːʊkʌst ɪn ðʌ ɹaŋ wɛːɪ]

[lɪp ˈɹaːʊndɪŋ ænd tʌŋ ˈfɹʌntɪŋ a ˈɛksɛlɛnt wɛːɪz tu ˈfoːʊkʌs ðʌ toːʊn]

[ˈfɔltɪ fɔˈmɛːɪʃʌnz ðæt ɪmˈpid ðʌ toːʊn ɪnˈklud]:

1. [loːʊ saft ˈpælæt (ˈnɛːɪzʊl toːʊn)]

2. [bæk tʌŋ aʧ (tʌŋ ɪmˈpidɛd toːʊn)]

3. [ʌnɹɪˈlist ʤɔ poˈzɪʃʌn (ˈlɪmɪtɛd pɹoˈʤɛkʃʌn ʌv ðʌ toːʊn)]

4. [smaːɪl (spɹɛd toːʊn)]

* *Replace* [з] *with a German vowel "r". This "r" is formed with the tongue tip down. Rounding the lips for* [з] *will help focus the tone.*

Notes

Personal Assessment

Breath
Breath Control   70-------------79/80-------------89/90-------------100
Breath Expansion   70-------------79/80-------------89/90-------------100
Breath Support   70-------------79/80-------------89/90-------------100

Diction
Consonant Articulation 70-------------79/80-------------89/90-------------100
Vowel Formation   70-------------79/80-------------89/90-------------100

Musicianship
Expression   70-------------79/80-------------89/90-------------100
Legato   70-------------79/80-------------89/90-------------100
Pitch Accuracy   70-------------79/80-------------89/90-------------100
Rhythmic Accuracy   70-------------79/80-------------89/90-------------100

Posture and Tension
Postural Alignment   70-------------79/80-------------89/90-------------100
Release of Tension   70-------------79/80-------------89/90-------------100

Technique
Flexibility   70-------------79/80-------------89/90-------------100
Onset   70-------------79/80-------------89/90-------------100
Palatal Space   70-------------79/80-------------89/90-------------100
Pharyngeal Space   70-------------79/80-------------89/90-------------100
Projection   70-------------79/80-------------89/90-------------100
Vibrato   70-------------79/80-------------89/90-------------100
Tone Quality   70-------------79/80-------------89/90-------------100
Vowel Equalization   70-------------79/80-------------89/90-------------100

Exploring Chiaroscuro – [y] and [ʏ]

[mɪkst ˈvaːʊʌlz gɪv ðʌ ˈsɪŋʌ ðʌ ˈbɛnɛfɪt ʌv ˈɹaːʊndɪŋ ænd ˈfɹʌntɪŋ]

[fɹʌnt ˈvaːʊʌlz ɪnˈhans fʌˈɹɪndʒʊl spɛːɪs ænd ˈbɹɪljænsɪ ʌv ðʌ toːʊn]

[bæk ˈvaːʊʌlz ɪnˈhans ˈfɔwʊd pɹoˈdʒɛkʃʌn ænd ˈɹɪtʃnɛs ʌv ðʌ toːʊn]

[mɪkst ˈvaːʊʌlz hæv ɔl ʌv ði ʌˈbʌv – ˈkjaroskuɾo]

[mɪkst ˈvaːʊʌlz a ˈhɛlpfʊl fɔ ˈsɪŋʌz hu ˈstɹʌgʊl wɪð ʌ ˈbɹɛθɪ toːʊn]

The [y] Vowel

[ði [y] ˈvaːʊʌl hæz ðʌ spɛːɪs ʌv [a] ðʌ tʌŋ ʌv [i] ænd ðʌ lɪp ʌv [u]]

[fɔm ðʌ ˈvaːʊʌlz ˈɜlɪ ænd mɛːɪnˈtɛːɪn ðʌ ˈklæɾɪtɪ ʌv boːʊθ ˈvaːʊʌlz]

The [ʏ] Vowel

[ði [ʏ] ˈvaːʊʌl hæz ðʌ spɛːɪs ʌv [a] ðʌ tʌŋ ʌv [ɪ] ænd ðʌ lɪp ʌv [ʊ]]

[fɔm ðʌ ˈvaːʊʌlz ˈɜlɪ ænd mɛːɪnˈtɛːɪn ðʌ ˈklæɾɪtɪ ʌv boːʊθ ˈvaːʊʌlz]

Warnings

[ʌ dɪˈlɛːɪd lɪp ˈɹaːʊndɪŋ wɪl ɹɪˈzʌlt ɪn dɪfθaŋaːɪzˈɛːɪʃʌn ʌv ðʌ ˈvaːʊʌl]

[du nat ʌˈdapt ði [y] fɔˈmɛːɪʃʌn fɔ ði [u] ˈvaːʊʌl]

[ʌˈvɔːɪd ʌ ˈnɛːɪzʊlaːɪzd toːʊn]

Exercise

Round early: [u – y – u – y – u]

[ʊ – ʏ – ʊ – ʏ – ʊ]

Notes

Personal Assessment

Breath

Breath Control	70-------------79/80-------------89/90-------------100		
Breath Expansion	70-------------79/80-------------89/90-------------100		
Breath Support	70-------------79/80-------------89/90-------------100		

Diction

Consonant Articulation 70-------------79/80-------------89/90-------------100
Vowel Formation 70-------------79/80-------------89/90-------------100

Musicianship

Expression 70-------------79/80-------------89/90-------------100
Legato 70-------------79/80-------------89/90-------------100
Pitch Accuracy 70-------------79/80-------------89/90-------------100
Rhythmic Accuracy 70-------------79/80-------------89/90-------------100

Posture and Tension

Postural Alignment 70-------------79/80-------------89/90-------------100
Release of Tension 70-------------79/80-------------89/90-------------100

Technique

Flexibility 70-------------79/80-------------89/90-------------100
Onset 70-------------79/80-------------89/90-------------100
Palatal Space 70-------------79/80-------------89/90-------------100
Pharyngeal Space 70-------------79/80-------------89/90-------------100
Projection 70-------------79/80-------------89/90-------------100
Vibrato 70-------------79/80-------------89/90-------------100
Tone Quality 70-------------79/80-------------89/90-------------100
Vowel Equalization 70-------------79/80-------------89/90-------------100

Exploring Chiaroscuro – [ø] and [œ]

[ði [ø] ˈvaːʊʌl ɪz dɪˈfaːɪnd ˈsɛpɹætlɪ fɔ fɹɛnʧ ænd ˈʤɜmæn]

[ðʌ fɔˈmɛːɪʃʌn ɪz aːɪˈdɛntɪkʊl – ðʌ ˈvaːʊʌl ˈkʌlɔɾ ɪz ˈdɪfɹɛnt]

[ˈʌðʌ ˈaːɪˈpiˈɛːɪ ˈsɪmbʊlz ˈɔlsoːʊ hæv ˈvæɾɪɪŋ pɹonʌnsɪˈɛːɪʃʌnz]

[ði ˈaːɪˈpiˈɛːɪ dʌz nat pɹoˈvaːɪd ʌ junɪˈvɜsʊl dɛfɪˈnɪʃʌn ʌv ðʌ saːʊndz]

[pɹonʌnsɪˈɛːɪʃʌn mʌst bi dɪˈfaːɪnd wɪðˈɪn ðʌ ɹɪˈspɛktɪv ˈlæŋgwæʤ]

The [ø] Vowel

[ði [ø] ˈvaːʊʌl hæz ðʌ spɛːɪs ʌv [a] ðʌ tʌŋ ʌv [e] ænd ðʌ lɪp ʌv [o]]

[ðɛːʌɾ ɪz æn ˈædɛd [ɜ] ˈkʌlɔ fɔ ðʌ ˈʤɜmæn [ø]]

[ðɛːʌɾ ɪz æn ˈædɛd [ʊ] ˈkʌlɔ fɔ ðʌ fɹɛnʧ [ø]]

[fɔm ðʌ ˈvaːʊʌlz ˈɜlɪ ænd mɛːɪnˈtɛːɪn ðʌ ˈklæɾɪtɪ ʌv boːʊθ ˈvaːʊʌlz]

The [œ] Vowel

[ði [œ] ˈvaːʊʌl hæz ðʌ spɛːɪs ʌv [a] tʌŋ ʌv [ɛ] ænd lɪp ʌv [ɔ]]

[ðɛːʌɾ ɪz æn ˈædɛd [ʊ] ˈkʌlɔ fɔ ðʌ fɹɛnʧ [œ]]

[fɔm ðʌ ˈvaːʊʌlz ˈɜlɪ ænd mɛːɪnˈtɛːɪn ðʌ ˈklæɾɪtɪ ʌv boːʊθ ˈvaːʊʌlz]

Exercise

Round early: [o – ø – o – ø – o]   [ɔ – œ – ɔ – œ – ɔ]

Consonant Chart

	Bilabial	Labiodental	Dental	Alveolar	Prepalatal	Palatal	Velar	Glottal
Speech Formation	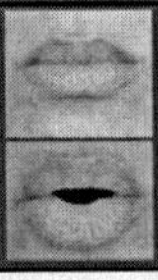	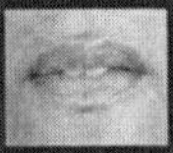	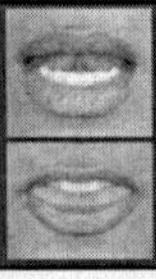	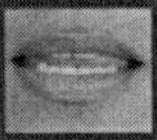	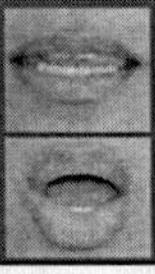	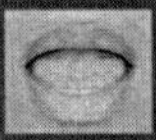		
Stop	[b] [p]		[d] [t]	[d] [t]			[g] [k]	[ʔ]
Fricative	[ʍ]	[v] [f]	[ð] [θ]	[z] [s]	[ʒ] [ʃ]	[ç]	[χ]	[h]
Affricate					[dʒ] [tʃ]			
Nasal	[m]			[n]	[ɲ]		[ŋ]	
Lateral			[l]	[l]	[ʎ]			
Glide	[w]				[ɥ]	[j]		
Trill			[ɾ]/[r]					
Retroflex				[ɹ]				

The consonants outside of the dark shaded box may be articulated with a lowered jaw position. Consonant terms are defined on page 153.

Consonant Articulation: Week 9

Day 1: Energizing the Diction

Day 2: Avoiding Consonant Entanglements

Day 3: Exploring Alternate Formations

Day 4: Consonant Parameters to Exclude

Day 5: Consonant Parameters to Explore

Day 6: Final Consonants and Consonant Clusters

Lesson Notes, Date: _________

Checklist of Concepts to Review

BREATH
Breath Control___
p: 35, 63, 67
Breath Support___
p: 63, 65
Breath Expansion___
p: 33, 35
DICTION
Articulation___
p: 121, 123, 125, 131
Front Vowels___
p: 57, 105
Back Vowels___
p: 73, 107
Central Vowels___
p: 89, 91, 93, 109, 111
Mixed Vowels___
p: 113, 115
FLEXIBILITY
Flexibility___
p: 109, 139
MUSICIANSHIP
Artistry___
p: 141
Dynamics___
p: 143
Legato___
p: 49, 59, 75, 139, 141

POSTURE
Postural Alignment___
p: 25, 27
RANGE
Range___
p: 81, 91, 139
TONE
Chiaroscuro___
p: 97, 113, 115
Lip Trills___
p: 41, 43
Palatal Resonance___
p: 89, 91, 93, 109
Pharyngeal Space___
p: 57, 59, 93, 105, 109
Projection___
p: 73, 75, 93, 107
Register___
p: 43, 83
Resonance___
p: 93, 95, 97, 109, 137
Sensory Awareness___
p: 61, 127
Vibrato___
p: 43, 45, 51, 77, 79, 81
Vowel Equalization___
p: 79, 95, 137
WARM-UPS___
p: 200-204

WARNINGS
Breathy Tone___
p: 35, 77, 113, 125, 127
Faulty Formation___
p. 111, 127
Faulty Movement___
p. 45, 47
Faulty Onset___
p: 59, 75, 127
Jaw Tension___
p: 31, 111, 121, 123, 125
Nasal Tone ___
p: 111, 127
Pressed Tone___
p: 35, 41, 43, 83
Spread Tone___
p: 57, 61, 73, 111
Tension___
p: 29, 31, 45, 47, 61
Tongue Impeded Tone___
p: 111, 127
OTHER
Choral Singing___
p: 99
Stage Deportment___
p: 145
Vocal health___
p: 147

Daily Notes and Practice Times

Day 1   Practice Time:__________

Day 2   Practice Time:__________

Day 3   Practice Time:__________

Day 4   Practice Time:__________

Day 5   Practice Time:__________

Day 6   Practice Time:__________

Notes

Personal Assessment

Breath
Breath Control   70-------------79/80-------------89/90-------------100
Breath Expansion   70-------------79/80-------------89/90-------------100
Breath Support   70-------------79/80-------------89/90-------------100

Diction
Consonant Articulation 70-------------79/80-------------89/90-------------100
Vowel Formation   70-------------79/80-------------89/90-------------100

Musicianship
Expression   70-------------79/80-------------89/90-------------100
Legato   70-------------79/80-------------89/90-------------100
Pitch Accuracy   70-------------79/80-------------89/90-------------100
Rhythmic Accuracy   70-------------79/80-------------89/90-------------100

Posture and Tension
Postural Alignment   70-------------79/80-------------89/90-------------100
Release of Tension   70-------------79/80-------------89/90-------------100

Technique
Flexibility   70-------------79/80-------------89/90-------------100
Onset   70-------------79/80-------------89/90-------------100
Palatal Space   70-------------79/80-------------89/90-------------100
Pharyngeal Space   70-------------79/80-------------89/90-------------100
Projection   70-------------79/80-------------89/90-------------100
Vibrato   70-------------79/80-------------89/90-------------100
Tone Quality   70-------------79/80-------------89/90-------------100
Vowel Equalization   70-------------79/80-------------89/90-------------100

Energizing the Diction

[ˈmænædʒɪŋ ˈvaːʊʌl/ˈkansonænt floːʊ ɪz ʌ ˈʧælendʒ fɔ ˈmɛnɪ ˈsɪŋʌz]

[ˈsɪŋɪŋ ɪz spɛːɪs – ˈkansonænts sim tu ʃʌt daːʊn ðæt spɛːɪs]

[hɪːʌɾ a tɪps fɔ ˈaptɪmaːɪzɪŋ ðʌ ˈmuvmɛnt fɹʌm ˈvaːʊʌl tu ˈkansonænt]:

1. [kip ði ɛːʌ ˈmuvɪŋ ʍaːɪl aˈtɪkjulɛːɪtɪŋ ˈkansonænts]

2. [θɪŋk ʌv ˈkansonænts æz ɛnʌˈdʒɛtɪk ɪntɹoˈdʌkʃʌnz tu ðʌ ˈvaːʊʌl]

3. [ðʌ ˈkantækt bɪˈtwin ði aˈtɪkjulɛːɪtʌz ʃʊd bi ˈdʒɛntʊl]

4. [aˈtɪkjulɛːɪt ɪn ʌ ˈɹæpɪd lɛːɪt ænd klɪːʌ ˈmænʌ]

5. [fɔm ðʌ ˈvaːʊʌl ˈɜlɪ ˈivɛn bɪˈfɔːʌ ˈkansonænt aˈtɪkjulɛːɪʃʌn]

6. [mɛːɪnˈtɛːɪn ðʌ ˈvaːʊʌl spɛːɪs ʍaːɪl aˈtɪkjulɛːɪtɪŋ ˈkansonænts]

Exercise

[ðʌ ˈfaloːʊɪŋ ˈɛksʌsaːɪz hɛlps ˈsɪŋʌz dɪsˈkʌvʌ ˈɛnʌdʒaːɪzd aˈtɪkjulɛːɪʃʌn]

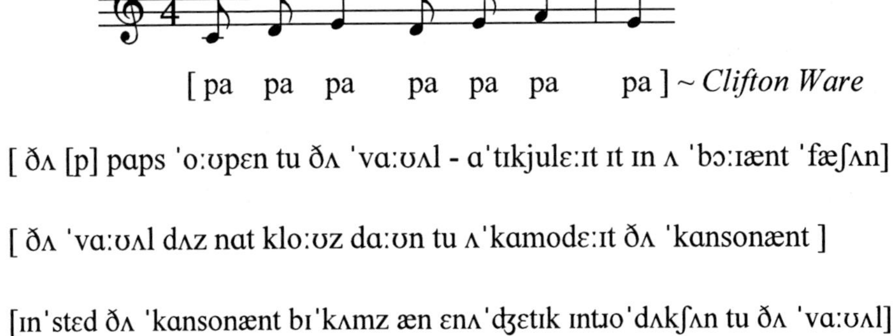

[ðʌ [p] paps ˈoːʊpɛn tu ðʌ ˈvaːʊʌl - aˈtɪkjulɛːɪt ɪt ɪn ʌ ˈbɔːɹænt ˈfæʃʌn]

[ðʌ ˈvaːʊʌl dʌz nat kloːʊz daːʊn tu ʌˈkamodɛːɪt ðʌ ˈkansonænt]

[ɪnˈstɛd ðʌ ˈkansonænt bɪˈkʌmz æn ɛnʌˈdʒɛtɪk ɪntɹoˈdʌkʃʌn tu ðʌ ˈvaːʊʌl]

[ʌˈplaːɪ ðʌ ˈɹæpɪd aˈtɪkjulʌtɔɾɪ ˈpɹapʌtɪz ʌv ʌ [p] tu ɔl ˈkansonænts]

Notes

Personal Assessment

Breath
Breath Control   70-------------79/80-------------89/90-------------100
Breath Expansion   70-------------79/80-------------89/90-------------100
Breath Support   70-------------79/80-------------89/90-------------100

Diction
Consonant Articulation 70-------------79/80-------------89/90-------------100
Vowel Formation   70-------------79/80-------------89/90-------------100

Musicianship
Expression   70-------------79/80-------------89/90-------------100
Legato   70-------------79/80-------------89/90-------------100
Pitch Accuracy   70-------------79/80-------------89/90-------------100
Rhythmic Accuracy   70-------------79/80-------------89/90-------------100

Posture and Tension
Postural Alignment   70-------------79/80-------------89/90-------------100
Release of Tension   70-------------79/80-------------89/90-------------100

Technique
Flexibility   70-------------79/80-------------89/90-------------100
Onset   70-------------79/80-------------89/90-------------100
Palatal Space   70-------------79/80-------------89/90-------------100
Pharyngeal Space   70-------------79/80-------------89/90-------------100
Projection   70-------------79/80-------------89/90-------------100
Vibrato   70-------------79/80-------------89/90-------------100
Tone Quality   70-------------79/80-------------89/90-------------100
Vowel Equalization   70-------------79/80-------------89/90-------------100

Avoiding Consonant Entanglements

[ˈdɪkʃʌn ɪz ʌ daːɹæɡˈnastɪk tul]

[klɪːʌ ˈdɪkʃʌn ɪz ˈɛvɪdɛns ʌv ˌʌnɪmˈpidɛd ˈvoːʊkʊl pɹoˈdʌkʃʌn]

[bɪˈɡɪnʌz aɾ ˈafɛn ˈkɹɪtɪsaːɪzd fɔ ˈʧuɪŋ ðɛːʌ wɜdz]

[ðɪs ɪz ʌˈvɔːɪdɛd baːɪ mɛːɪnˈtɛːɪnɪŋ ˈvaːʊʌl spɛːɪs ˈdjuːʌɾɪŋ aˈtɪkjulɛːɪʃʌn]

Intoning Exercise

[ðʌ ˈfaloːʊɪŋ ˈɛksʌsaːɪz pɹoˈvaːɪdz ˈkantɹastɪŋ aˈtɪkjulʌtɔɾɪ pɔːɪnts]

[mɛːɪnˈtɛːɪn ðʌ spɛːɪs ʌv [a] ʍaːɪl aˈtɪkjulɛːɪtɪŋ ðʌ ˈkansonænts]

[du nat ʌˈlaːʊ ðʌ ˈkansonænts tu ˈɔltʌ ðʌ ˈvaːʊʌl ˈkwalɪtɪ]

Bilabial and Alveolar	Labiodental and Palatal	Dental and Velar
[a b a]	[a v a]	[a ð a]
[a n a]	[a j a]	[a ŋ a]
[a p a]	[a f a]	[a θ a]
[a d a]	[a ç a]	[a g a]
[a m a]		[a l a]
[a t a]		[a k a]
[a w a]		[a ɾ a]
		[a x a]

> Do not curl the lips inward for *b*, *p*, or *m*. The inside of the lower lip contacts the outer ridge of the upper front teeth for *f* and *v*. Extend the tongue for *th*.

Articulatory Aid

[snæp af ðʌ ɹɪm ʌv ʌ ˈstaːɪɾofoːʊm kʌp]

[pɹɑp ʌ smɔl ˈsɛkʃʌn bɪˈtwin ðʌ fɹʌnt tiθ]

This acts as a spacer allowing the singer to maintain the vowel space while articulating consonants. Many teachers recommend the use of a cork for the same purpose. Warning: choking hazard.

Notes

Personal Assessment

Breath
Breath Control   70--------------79/80--------------89/90-------------100
Breath Expansion   70-------------79/80-------------89/90-------------100
Breath Support   70-------------79/80-------------89/90-------------100

Diction
Consonant Articulation 70-------------79/80--------------89/90-------------100
Vowel Formation   70-------------79/80-------------89/90-------------100

Musicianship
Expression   70-------------79/80--------------89/90-------------100
Legato   70-------------79/80--------------89/90-------------100
Pitch Accuracy   70-------------79/80--------------89/90-------------100
Rhythmic Accuracy   70-------------79/80--------------89/90-------------100

Posture and Tension
Postural Alignment 70--------------79/80--------------89/90-------------100
Release of Tension 70--------------79/80--------------89/90-------------100

Technique
Flexibility   70-------------79/80--------------89/90-------------100
Onset   70-------------79/80--------------89/90-------------100
Palatal Space   70-------------79/80--------------89/90-------------100
Pharyngeal Space   70-------------79/80--------------89/90-------------100
Projection   70--------------79/80--------------89/90-------------100
Vibrato   70-------------79/80--------------89/90-------------100
Tone Quality   70-------------79/80--------------89/90-------------100
Vowel Equalization 70-------------79/80--------------89/90-------------100

Exploring Alternate Consonant Formations

[ˈkansonænt aˈtɪkjulɛːɪʃʌn ʃʊd nat dɪsˈɹʌpt ðʌ ˈvaːʊʌl spɛːɪs]

[ˈsɜtæn ˈkansonænts du nat ʌˈkamodɛːɪt ʌ ɹɪˈlist ʤɔ poˈzɪʃʌn]

[ðiz ˈkansonænts ɪnˈklud [z] [s] [ʒ] ænd [ʃ] (si pɛːɪʤ ˈwʌnsɪkstin)]

[ðɛːɪ aɾ aˈtɪkjulɛːɪtɛd wɪð ðʌ tʌŋ tɪp ɪn ʌ kloːʊzd ʤɔ poˈzɪʃʌn]

[ɪkˈsploːʌɾ æn ˈɔltʌnæt fɔˈmɛːɪʃʌn baːɪ aˈtɪkjulɛːɪtɪŋ ðɛm wɪð ðʌ tʌŋ aʧ]

[ˈɔltʌnæt ˈkansonænt fɔˈmɛːɪʃʌnz ˈsɪmplɪfaːɪ ði aˈtɪkjulʌtɔɾɪ ˈpɹasɛs]

As a general rule, any consonant (except r) may be articulated with the tongue tip contacting the lower front teeth.

[ðɪs ɪz ˈmɪːʌlɪ æn ˈapʃʌn tu ɪkˈsploːʌ]

[ˈɛnɪ fɔˈmɛːɪʃʌn ðæt dɪsˈtɔts ðʌ ˈklæɾɪtɪ ʌv ðʌ tɛkst ɪz nat ɹɛkʌˈmɛndɛd]

Exploring Alternate Vowel Formations

[ˈvaːʊʌl madɪtɪˈkɛːɪʃʌn ˈɔltʌz ðʌ ʃɛːɪp ʌv ʌ ˈvaːʊʌl tu ɪkˈspænd ðʌ spɛːɪs]

[vaːʊʌl maːɪˈgɹɛːɪʃʌn ɹɪˈtɛːɪnz ðʌ ˈfoːʊkʌs ʌv kloːʊzd vaːʊʌlz -pɛːɪʤ 100]

[ˈklæɾɪfaːɪ ʌ ˈbɹɛθɪ [ɛ] baːɪ fɔmɪŋ ɪt wɪð æn [i] tʌŋ <u>ɪn ði [a] spɛːɪs</u>]

[ˈklæɾɪfaːɪ ʌ ˈbɹɛθɪ [a] baːɪ fɔmɪŋ ɪt wɪð æn [ɔ] lɪp <u>ɪn ði [a] spɛːɪs</u>]

[ðɪs ɪz ˈmɪːʌlɪ æn ˈapʃʌn tu ɪkˈsploːʌ]

[ˈɛnɪ fɔˈmɛːɪʃʌn ðæt dɪsˈtɔts ðʌ ˈklæɾɪtɪ ʌv ðʌ tɛkst ɪz nat ɹɛkʌˈmɛndɛd]

Notes

Personal Assessment

Breath

Breath Control　　　　70-------------79/80-------------89/90-------------100
Breath Expansion　　　70-------------79/80-------------89/90-------------100
Breath Support　　　　70-------------79/80-------------89/90-------------100

Diction

Consonant Articulation　70-------------79/80-------------89/90-------------100
Vowel Formation　　　　70-------------79/80-------------89/90-------------100

Musicianship

Expression　　　　　　70-------------79/80-------------89/90-------------100
Legato　　　　　　　　70-------------79/80-------------89/90-------------100
Pitch Accuracy　　　　70-------------79/80-------------89/90-------------100
Rhythmic Accuracy　　70-------------79/80-------------89/90-------------100

Posture and Tension

Postural Alignment　　70-------------79/80-------------89/90-------------100
Release of Tension　　70-------------79/80-------------89/90-------------100

Technique

Flexibility　　　　　　70-------------79/80-------------89/90-------------100
Onset　　　　　　　　70-------------79/80-------------89/90-------------100
Palatal Space　　　　　70-------------79/80-------------89/90-------------100
Pharyngeal Space　　　70-------------79/80-------------89/90-------------100
Projection　　　　　　70-------------79/80-------------89/90-------------100
Vibrato　　　　　　　70-------------79/80-------------89/90-------------100
Tone Quality　　　　　70-------------79/80-------------89/90-------------100
Vowel Equalization　　70-------------79/80-------------89/90-------------100

Consonants as Diagnostic Tools

[ˈkansonænts kæn bi juzd tu dɪsˈkʌvʌ ˈværɪʌs ˈɹɛzonænt ʃɛːɪps]

[ðɛːɪ ɑ ˈjusfʊl fɔr ɛksplɔˈɹɛːɪʃʌn ˈoːʊnlɪ sɪns ðɛːɪ ˈmɪnɪmɑːɪz ðʌ spɛːɪs]

[ˈɑptɪmʊl toːʊn kæn ˈoːʊnlɪ ʌˈkɜɾ ɪn ðʌ tɔl spɛːɪs ðæt ˈvɑːʊʌlz pɹoˈvɑːɪd]

[ɪkˈsplɔːʌɾɪŋ ˈkansonænt fɔˈmɛːɪʃʌn ɪz bɛnɪˈfɪʃʊl fɔ ˈtæktɪl ˈpɜpʌsɛz]

[ˈkansonænts kæn ˈɔlsoːʊ sɜv æz ɪgˈzampʊlz ʌv ʌ ˈfɔltɪ toːʊn]

When a student is unable to find adequate space; a consonant point or manner of articulation can be used to describe the "where not to go" before optimal is discovered.

Consonant Parameters to Exclude

[ðʌ ˈdɑːɹʌgɹæm bɪˈloːʊ dɪˈfɑːɪnz ðʌ ˈdɛːɪndʒʌ zoːʊnz fɔr ʌ ˈsɪŋʌ]

[ʌ [h] ˈmænʌɾ ʌv aˈtɪkjulɛːɪʃʌn ˈmɪmɪks ðʌ ˈkwalɪtɪ ʌv ʌ ˈbɹɛθɪ toːʊn]

[ðʌ [ʔ] pɔːɪnt ʌv aˈtɪkjulɛːɪʃʌn ˈɹɛplɪkɛːɪts ði ˈansɛt ʌv ʌ ˈθɹoːʊtɪ toːʊn]

[ʌ [m] ˈmænʌɾ ʌv ɑˈtɪkjulɛːɪʃʌn ˈdɛmʌnstɹɛːɪts ʌ ˈnɛːɪzʊl toːʊn]

[ˈvilʌ ˈkansonænts hæv ʌ tʌŋ fɔˈmɛːɪʃʌn ðæt ɪmˈpidz ðʌ toːʊn]

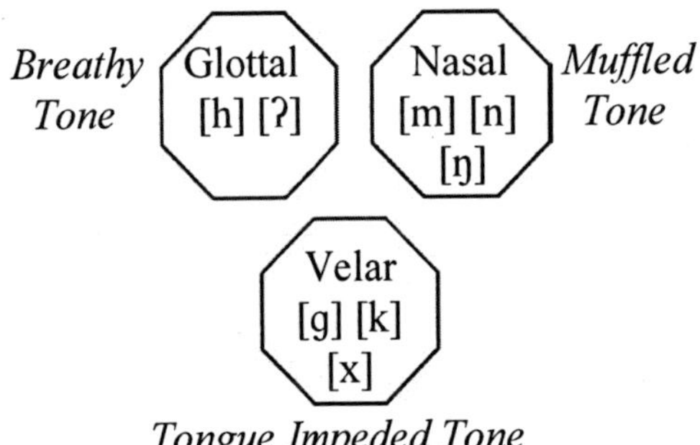

Tongue Impeded Tone

Monitor the quality of the tone by pinching the nostrils together while singing. The flow of air is nasal if this further muffles the sound.

Notes

Personal Assessment

Breath
Breath Control   70-------------79/80-------------89/90-------------100
Breath Expansion   70-------------79/80-------------89/90-------------100
Breath Support   70-------------79/80-------------89/90-------------100

Diction
Consonant Articulation 70-------------79/80-------------89/90-------------100
Vowel Formation   70-------------79/80-------------89/90-------------100

Musicianship
Expression   70-------------79/80-------------89/90-------------100
Legato   70-------------79/80-------------89/90-------------100
Pitch Accuracy   70-------------79/80-------------89/90-------------100
Rhythmic Accuracy   70-------------79/80-------------89/90-------------100

Posture and Tension
Postural Alignment   70-------------79/80-------------89/90-------------100
Release of Tension   70-------------79/80-------------89/90-------------100

Technique
Flexibility   70-------------79/80-------------89/90-------------100
Onset   70-------------79/80-------------89/90-------------100
Palatal Space   70-------------79/80-------------89/90-------------100
Pharyngeal Space   70-------------79/80-------------89/90-------------100
Projection   70-------------79/80-------------89/90-------------100
Vibrato   70-------------79/80-------------89/90-------------100
Tone Quality   70-------------79/80-------------89/90-------------100
Vowel Equalization   70-------------79/80-------------89/90-------------100

Consonant Parameters to Explore

[ðʌ tʌŋ ænd lɪps ɑ ˈlɛːɪzɪ ɪn ðʌ ˈspikʌz mɑːʊθ]

Good diction is the result of flexibility of the tongue and the lip and the independent action of the tongue from the jaw. Barbara Honn

[ðʌ ˈsɪŋʌz aˈtɪkjulɛːɪtɔz mʌst bi tɹɛːɪnd tu fɔm ˈvaːʊʌlz ˈækjʊɾætlɪ]

[ˈkansonænts pɹoˈvaːɪd ɪgˈzampʊlz ʌv ɪkˈstɹim ˈfɹʌntɪŋ ɔ ˈɹaːʊndɪŋ]

Explanation of the Diagram

[ðʌ ˈsɪmbʊlz ɪn ðʌ ˈsɜkʊlz gɪv æn ɪgˈzædʒʌˌɾɛːɪtɛd ˈmadʊl fɔ ˈvaːʊʌlz]

[ðʌ ˈsɪmbʊlz ɪn ˈbaksɛz pɹoˈvaːɪd ʌ ˈvɔːɪslɛs ˈsampʊlɪŋ ʌv ɔl fɔˈmɛːɪʃʌnz]

[ðʌ tʌŋ aʃ kæn bi fɛlt baːɪ ˈʍɪspʌɾɪŋ ðʌ ˈsɪmbʊlz ɪn ðʌ ˈbaksɛz]

Note: [ðʌ [h] ˈkansonænt ʌˈdapts ðʌ fɔˈmɛːɪʃʌn ʌv ʌ ˈfalɔːʊɪŋ ˈvaːʊʌl]

[ˈaptɪmʊl ˈɔɾʊl spɛːɪs ɪz ʌˈʧivd wɪð ðʌ [h] ʌv hat ɔ hap]

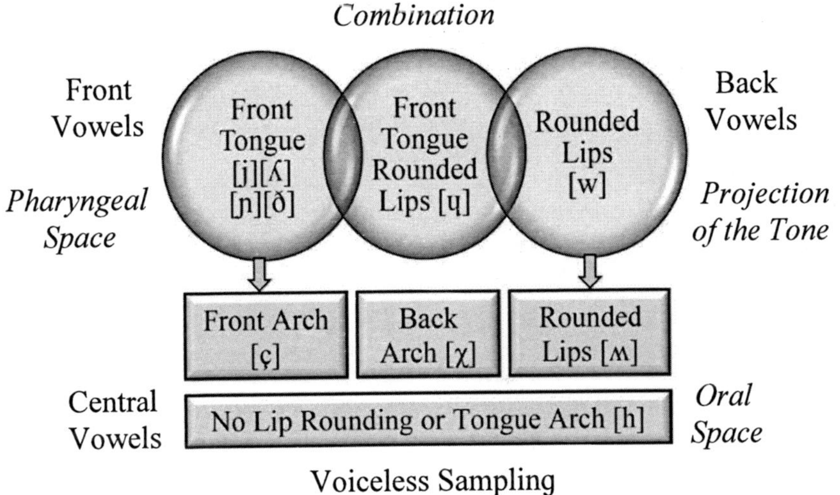

Notes

Personal Assessment

Breath
Breath Control   70--------------79/80-------------89/90------------100
Breath Expansion   70--------------79/80-------------89/90------------100
Breath Support   70--------------79/80-------------89/90------------100

Diction
Consonant Articulation 70--------------79/80-------------89/90------------100
Vowel Formation   70--------------79/80-------------89/90------------100

Musicianship
Expression   70--------------79/80-------------89/90------------100
Legato   70--------------79/80-------------89/90------------100
Pitch Accuracy   70--------------79/80-------------89/90------------100
Rhythmic Accuracy   70--------------79/80-------------89/90------------100

Posture and Tension
Postural Alignment   70--------------79/80-------------89/90------------100
Release of Tension   70--------------79/80-------------89/90------------100

Technique
Flexibility   70--------------79/80-------------89/90------------100
Onset   70--------------79/80-------------89/90------------100
Palatal Space   70--------------79/80-------------89/90------------100
Pharyngeal Space   70--------------79/80-------------89/90------------100
Projection   70--------------79/80-------------89/90------------100
Vibrato   70--------------79/80-------------89/90------------100
Tone Quality   70--------------79/80-------------89/90------------100
Vowel Equalization   70--------------79/80-------------89/90------------100

Final Consonants

[ði aˈtɪkjulɛːɪtɔz hæv ʌ ˈgɹɛːɪtʌ ˈdɪstæns tu ˈtɹævʊl ɪn ðʌ ˈsɪŋʌz mɑːʊθ]

[aˈtɪkjulɛːɪʃʌn mʌst bi kwɪk soːʊ ˈvɑːʊʌl spɛːɪs kæn ɹɪˈmɛːɪn ʌndɪˈstɜbd]

[du nat aˈtɪkjulɛːɪt ðʌ ˈkansonænt ˈɜlɪ nɔɾ ʌˈlɑːʊ ɪt tu ˈkʌlɔ ðʌ ˈvɑːʊʌl]

Consonant Clusters

[iʧ ˈkansonænt ɪn ʌ ˈklʌstʌ mʌst bi mɜdʒd wɪð ðʌ ˈfaloːʊɪŋ sɑːʊnd]

[ʌˈvɔːɪd ˌɪntʌˈvinɪŋ ˈvɑːʊʌlz ɔ klɪks ʌv ðʌ tʌŋ ɔ lɪps]

[du nat oˈmɪt ˈkansonænts fɹʌm ˈkansonænt ˈklʌstʌz]

[ˈfʊlɪ vɔːɪs vɔːɪst ˈkansonænts ænd ˈfʊlɪ æspɪˈɾɛːɪt ˈvɔːɪslɛs ˈkansonænts]

[fɔ ˈdɪfɪkʊlt kambɪˈnɛːɪʃʌnz ɪˈlaŋgɛːɪt ðʌ kʌnˈtɪnjuænts ænd mɜdʒ ɔl]

Challenging Consonant Clusters

[bd]: sobbed, subdue
[blst]: humbl'st, troubl'st
[bz]: webs, herbs
[dst]: didst, amidst
[dz]: shades, clouds
[dʒd]: changed, pledged
[fnz]: deaf'ns, soft'ns
[fs]: griefs, cliffs
[fst]: scoff'st, laugh'st
[gd]: begged, flogged
[gl]: gleam, glad
[gz]: leagues, dogs
[kst]: next, ecstacy
[kt]: act, looked
[kts]: respects, facts

[lbz]: bulbs
[ldz]: fields, gilds
[ldʒd]: indulged
[lf]: self, skillful
[lfs]: elf's, wolf's
[lft]: engulfed
[lks]: silks, elks
[lm]: realm, almost
[lmd]: calmed, filmed
[lmz]: films, elms
[lps]: helps, whelps
[lst]: dwell'st, fill'st
[lt]: vault, felt
[lts]: melts, waltz
[lvd]: resolved, involved

Challenging Consonant Clusters

[lvz]: elves, shelves
[lz]: bells, calls
[mf]: comfort, triumph
[mfs]: triumphs, nymphs
[mps]: lamps, glimpse
[mst]: seem'st
[mz]: charms, dreams
[ndz]: sands, winds
[ndʒ]: angel, strange
[ndʒd]: changed, plunged
[ns]: once, dance
[nst]: against, constant
[nt]: plant, grant
[nts]: saints, moments
[ntʃ]: French, ancient
[ntʃt]: launched, quenched
[nz]: shines, runs
[ŋ]: sing, young
[ŋk]: drink, tranquil
[ŋks]: winks, thanks
[ŋkʃ]: anxious

[ŋkt]: adjunct
[ŋz]: songs, wings
[ps]: lips, keeps
[pt]: wept, stopped
[pts]: accepts, attempts
[sf]: sphinx, sphere
[sk]: sky, dusk
[sks]: asks, desks
[skt]: asked, risked
[sm]: smile, smart
[spl]: splendid, displeasure
[sps]: gasps, lisps
[spt]: clasped, grasped
[st]: still, stay
[sts]: mists, tempests
[ts]: lights, streets
[tst]: footsteps, outstretched
[tʃt]: matched, watched
[vd]: believed, braved
[vn]: heav'n, ev'n
[vz]: loves, gives

Clusters with *th*: Extend the tongue tip beyond the upper front teeth and draw it in gently while enunciating all consonants in the cluster.

[ðd]: breathed, loathed
[ðz]: youths, truths
[dθ]: breadth, width
[fθs]: fifths, twelfths
[lθ]: health, wealth
[lθf]: healthful
[lθs]: health's, wealth's

[nθ]: seventh, anthem
[nθs]: months, tenths
[ŋθs]: lengths, strength's
[pθs]: depths
[θn]: length'n, strength'n
[θɾ]: thread, throne
[θs]: youth's, faiths

Clusters with *r*: Pronounce all consonants with the lip rounding of *r*.

[bɹ]: bright, breath
[dɹ]: dream, wondrous
[fɹ]: friend, fragrant
[gɹ]: grace, green
[kɹ]: create, secret

[pɹ]: praise, pretty
[spɹ]: spring, spray
[stɹ]: strength, stream
[ʃɹ]: shroud, shrine
[tɹ]: tree, trim

Musicianship and Performance: Week 10

Day 1: Vowel Equalization

Day 2: Exploring Range and Flexibility

Day 3: Discovering Artistry

Day 4: Dynamic Control

Day 5: Stage Deportment

Day 6: Vocal Health

Lesson Notes, Date: _____________

Checklist of Concepts to Review

BREATH
Breath Control___
p: 35, 63, 67
Breath Support___
p: 63, 65
Breath Expansion___
p: 33, 35
DICTION
Articulation___
p: 121, 123, 125, 131
Front Vowels___
p: 57, 105
Back Vowels___
p: 73, 107
Central Vowels___
p: 89, 91, 93, 109, 111
Mixed Vowels___
p: 113, 115
FLEXIBILITY
Flexibility___
p: 109, 139
MUSICIANSHIP
Artistry___
p: 141
Dynamics___
p: 143
Legato___
p: 49, 59, 75, 139, 141

POSTURE
Postural Alignment___
p: 25, 27
RANGE
Range___
p: 81, 91, 139
TONE
Chiaroscuro___
p: 97, 113, 115
Lip Trills___
p: 41, 43
Palatal Resonance___
p: 89, 91, 93, 109
Pharyngeal Space___
p: 57, 59, 93, 105, 109
Projection___
p: 73, 75, 93, 107
Register___
p: 43, 83
Resonance___
p: 93, 95, 97, 109, 137
Sensory Awareness___
p: 61, 127
Vibrato___
p: 43, 45, 51, 77, 79, 81
Vowel Equalization___
p: 79, 95, 137
WARM-UPS___
p: 200-204

WARNINGS
Breathy Tone___
p: 35, 77, 113, 125, 127
Faulty Formation___
p. 111, 127
Faulty Movement___
p. 45, 47
Faulty Onset___
p: 59, 75, 127
Jaw Tension___
p: 31, 111, 121, 123, 125
Nasal Tone ___
p: 111, 127
Pressed Tone___
p: 35, 41, 43, 83
Spread Tone___
p: 57, 61, 73, 111
Tension___
p: 29, 31, 45, 47, 61
Tongue Impeded Tone___
p: 111, 127
OTHER
Choral Singing___
p: 99
Stage Deportment___
p: 145
Vocal health___
p: 147

Daily Notes and Practice Times

Day 1   Practice Time:__________

Day 2   Practice Time:__________

Day 3   Practice Time:__________

Day 4   Practice Time:__________

Day 5   Practice Time:__________

Day 6   Practice Time:__________

Notes

Personal Assessment

Breath
Breath Control   70--------------79/80--------------89/90--------------100
Breath Expansion   70--------------79/80--------------89/90--------------100
Breath Support   70--------------79/80--------------89/90--------------100

Diction
Consonant Articulation 70--------------79/80--------------89/90--------------100
Vowel Formation   70--------------79/80--------------89/90--------------100

Musicianship
Expression   70--------------79/80--------------89/90--------------100
Legato   70--------------79/80--------------89/90--------------100
Pitch Accuracy   70--------------79/80--------------89/90--------------100
Rhythmic Accuracy   70--------------79/80--------------89/90--------------100

Posture and Tension
Postural Alignment   70--------------79/80--------------89/90--------------100
Release of Tension   70--------------79/80--------------89/90--------------100

Technique
Flexibility   70--------------79/80--------------89/90--------------100
Onset   70--------------79/80--------------89/90--------------100
Palatal Space   70--------------79/80--------------89/90--------------100
Pharyngeal Space   70--------------79/80--------------89/90--------------100
Projection   70--------------79/80--------------89/90--------------100
Vibrato   70--------------79/80--------------89/90--------------100
Tone Quality   70--------------79/80--------------89/90--------------100
Vowel Equalization   70--------------79/80--------------89/90--------------100

Vowel Equalization

Vowels are equalized when the singer discovers the ability to maintain consistent resonance throughout all vowel formations.

Review: [ˈɹɛzonæns ɪz ʃɛːɪp ɔɹɪɛnˈtɛːɪʃʌn ænd ˈmuvmɛnt]

[ʃɛːɪp ɹɪˈfɜz tu ˈvɑːʊʌl fɔˈmɛːɪʃʌn (iʧ ˈvɑːʊʌl hæz ʌ juˈnik ʃɛːɪp)]

[ɔɹɪɛnˈtɛːɪʃʌn ɹɪˈfɜz tu ɛːʌ floːʊ (fɔm ðʌ ʃɛːɪp ænd spɪn bɪˈjɑnd ɪt)]

[ˈmuvmɛnt ɪz ˈvɑːɪbɹænsɪ (toːʊn ʃɛːɪp ænd ɔɹɪɛnˈtɛːɪʃʌn wɜk tuˈgɛðʌ)]

Know Your Voice

[ˈvɑːʊʌl ikwʊlɑːɪˈzɛːɪʃʌn ɪz bɛːɪst ɑn ðʌ ˈɹɛzonæns ʌv ˈɑptɪmʊl "ah"]

[ˈɑptɪmʊl "ah" mɛːɪ bi pɜˈsivd bɑːɪ ðʌ ˈsɪŋʌɹ æz [ɑ] [ɑ] ɔɾ ˈivɛn [ɔ]]

[ɪt ʌˈlɑːɪnz wɪð ʌ ˈsɪŋʌz juˈnik ˈfɛːɪʃʊl ˈstɹʌkʧʊɾ ænd ˈɹɛzonænt spɛːɪs]

[ɔl ˈvɑːʊʌlz hʊk ˈɪntu ðʌ sɛːɪm ˈɹɛzonænt kɔːʌ wʌns "ah" ɪz ˈɑptɪmɑːɪzd]

Exercise

[sɪˈlɛkt jɔːʌ vɔːɪsɪz moːʊst ˈɹɛzonænt ˈvɑːʊʌl [u] [i] [a] [ɑ] [ɔ]]

[ɪnˈtoːʊn ðʌ ˈsikwɛns ðæt kɔɾɛsˈpɑndz wɪð jɔːʌ bɛst ˈvɑːʊʌl]:

    [u]: [u] [o] [a] [e] [i]

    [i]: [i] [e] [a] [o] [u]

    [a]: [i] [e] [a] [o] [u]

    [ɑ]: [u] [o] [a] [e] [i]

    [ɔ]: [u] [o] [a] [e] [i]

Notes

Personal Assessment

Breath
Breath Control   70-------------79/80-------------89/90-------------100
Breath Expansion   70-------------79/80-------------89/90-------------100
Breath Support   70-------------79/80-------------89/90-------------100

Diction
Consonant Articulation   70-------------79/80-------------89/90-------------100
Vowel Formation   70-------------79/80-------------89/90-------------100

Musicianship
Expression   70-------------79/80-------------89/90-------------100
Legato   70-------------79/80-------------89/90-------------100
Pitch Accuracy   70-------------79/80-------------89/90-------------100
Rhythmic Accuracy   70-------------79/80-------------89/90-------------100

Posture and Tension
Postural Alignment   70-------------79/80-------------89/90-------------100
Release of Tension   70-------------79/80-------------89/90-------------100

Technique
Flexibility   70-------------79/80-------------89/90-------------100
Onset   70-------------79/80-------------89/90-------------100
Palatal Space   70-------------79/80-------------89/90-------------100
Pharyngeal Space   70-------------79/80-------------89/90-------------100
Projection   70-------------79/80-------------89/90-------------100
Vibrato   70-------------79/80-------------89/90-------------100
Tone Quality   70-------------79/80-------------89/90-------------100
Vowel Equalization   70-------------79/80-------------89/90-------------100

Exploring Range and Flexibility

[flɛksɪ'bɪlɪtɪ ɾɪ'kwaːɹʌz lɪ'gatoːʊ 'tɜnʌɾaːʊndz ænd noːʊt 'gɾupɪŋz]

Legato

[bɹɛːɪks ɪn ðʌ lɪ'gatoːʊ ɑ ði 'ɛnɪmɪ ʌv flɛksɪ'bɪlɪtɪ]

[klɪks ɪn ðʌ laːɪn wɛːɪst ɛːʌr ænd tɹɪp ʌp ðʌ 'sɪŋʌ]

Turnarounds

[ʌ 'tɜnʌɾaːʊnd ʌ'kɜz ʍɛn ʌ skɛːɪl ɹɪ'vɜsɛz daːɪ'ɾɛkʃʌnz]

['nɛːɪzʊl 'kansonænts ʌ'sɪst wɪð 'muvɪŋ ðʌ vɔːɪs]

['mastʌ ðʌ 'faloːʊɪŋ 'tɜnʌɾaːʊndz ɪn 'væɾɪʌs 'tɛmpi]

[du nat ʌ'laːʊ ðʌ 'nɛːɪzʊl 'kansonænt tu 'kʌlɔ ðʌ 'vaːʊʌl]:

[ðʌ 'sɪŋʌɾ ɪz 'ɹɛdɪ fɔ skɛːɪlz ʍʌns ðʌ noːʊts ɑ 'ɹɪðmɪklɪ 'ivɛn]

Note Groupings

['ɔgænaːɪz ðʌ noːʊts ʌv ðʌ naːɪn toːʊn skɛːɪl 'ɪntu gɾups ʌv fɔːʌ]

[ɪn'ɪʃiɛːɪt bɹɛθ sʌ'pɔt an ðʌ fɜst noːʊt ʌv ɪʃ gɾup ʌv fɔːʌ]:

Notes

Personal Assessment

Breath
Breath Control   70-------------79/80-------------89/90-------------100
Breath Expansion   70-------------79/80-------------89/90-------------100
Breath Support   70-------------79/80-------------89/90-------------100

Diction
Consonant Articulation   70-------------79/80-------------89/90-------------100
Vowel Formation   70-------------79/80-------------89/90-------------100

Musicianship
Expression   70-------------79/80-------------89/90-------------100
Legato   70-------------79/80-------------89/90-------------100
Pitch Accuracy   70-------------79/80-------------89/90-------------100
Rhythmic Accuracy   70-------------79/80-------------89/90-------------100

Posture and Tension
Postural Alignment   70-------------79/80-------------89/90-------------100
Release of Tension   70-------------79/80-------------89/90-------------100

Technique
Flexibility   70-------------79/80-------------89/90-------------100
Onset   70-------------79/80-------------89/90-------------100
Palatal Space   70-------------79/80-------------89/90-------------100
Pharyngeal Space   70-------------79/80-------------89/90-------------100
Projection   70-------------79/80-------------89/90-------------100
Vibrato   70-------------79/80-------------89/90-------------100
Tone Quality   70-------------79/80-------------89/90-------------100
Vowel Equalization   70-------------79/80-------------89/90-------------100

Discovering Artistry

[ˈɑtɪstɹɪ ɪz ðʌ ˈskɪlfʊl ɪkˈspɹɛʃʌn ʌv tɛkst ænd ˈmjuzɪk]

[ˈbɛːɪsɪk mjuˈzɪʃænʃɪp ɪnˈvɑlvz ˈækjʊɾæsɪ ʌv ˈɹɪðʌm ænd pɪʧ]

[ædˈvanst mjuˈzɪʃænʃɪp ɪnˈvɑlvz lɪˈgatoːʊ ˈfɹɛːɪzɪŋ ænd dɑːɪˈnæmɪks]

Legato

[lɪˈgatoːʊ kʌˈnɛkʃʌn gɪvz ðʌ ˈsɪŋʌ ðʌ ˈfɹidʌm tu ʃɛːɪp ðʌ fɹɛːɪz]

[dɹoːʊn spɪʧ hɛlps ðʌ ˈsɪŋʌ dɪsˈkʌvʌɾ ʌ lɪˈgatoːʊ ɪnʌnsɪˈɛːɪʃʌn ʌv ðʌ tɛkst]

[spik ðʌ tɛkst wɪð laŋ ˈvaːʊʌlz ænd lɛːɪt ˈɹæpɪd ænd klɪːʌ ˈkansonænts]

[ðɪs kʌmˈpɛlz ðʌ ˈsɪŋʌ tu ˈlɪŋgʌɾ an ðʌ ˈvaːʊʌl ænd ɹʌʃ ðʌ ˈkansonænt]

Phrasing

[ˈʃɛːɪpɪŋ ðʌ fɹɛːɪz ɹɪˈkwaːɪʌz æn ʌndʌˈstændɪŋ ʌv ðʌ tɛkst ænd ˈmjuzɪk]

[ði ˈatɪst ˈdɪlɪʤɛntlɪ ɹɪˈsɜʧɛz ˈpoːʊɛt kʌmˈpoːʊzʌɾ ænd tɛkst]

[ˈfɹɛːɪzɪŋ ɪnˈvɑlvz daːɪˈɾɛkʃʌn æz wɛl]:

[ði ɪnˈtaːɪʌ fɹɛːɪz ʃʊd bi ɪn ðʌ ˈsɪŋʌz maːɪnd bɪˈfɔːʌ ði ˈansɛt]

[ðʌ bɹɛθ ɪz ˈmɛʒʊd baːɪ ðʌ fɹɛːɪz ænd bɪˈkʌmz ɪts ɪnspɪˈɾɛːɪʃʌn]

[ðʌ last wɜd ʌv ʌ fɹɛːɪz ˈɪndɪkɛːɪts ðʌ daːɪˈɾɛkʃʌn – sɪŋ twɔd ɪt]

Dynamics

Dynamic control (crescendo and decrescendo) is the last skill studied in the bel canto style. Phrasing requires dynamic control which is guided by an intimate understanding of the text and music.

Notes

Personal Assessment

Breath

Breath Control   70-------------79/80-------------89/90-------------100
Breath Expansion   70-------------79/80-------------89/90-------------100
Breath Support   70-------------79/80-------------89/90-------------100

Diction

Consonant Articulation   70-------------79/80-------------89/90-------------100
Vowel Formation   70-------------79/80-------------89/90-------------100

Musicianship

Expression   70-------------79/80-------------89/90-------------100
Legato   70-------------79/80-------------89/90-------------100
Pitch Accuracy   70-------------79/80-------------89/90-------------100
Rhythmic Accuracy   70-------------79/80-------------89/90-------------100

Posture and Tension

Postural Alignment   70-------------79/80-------------89/90-------------100
Release of Tension   70-------------79/80-------------89/90-------------100

Technique

Flexibility   70-------------79/80-------------89/90-------------100
Onset   70-------------79/80-------------89/90-------------100
Palatal Space   70-------------79/80-------------89/90-------------100
Pharyngeal Space   70-------------79/80-------------89/90-------------100
Projection   70-------------79/80-------------89/90-------------100
Vibrato   70-------------79/80-------------89/90-------------100
Tone Quality   70-------------79/80-------------89/90-------------100
Vowel Equalization   70-------------79/80-------------89/90-------------100

Dynamic Control

[dɑːɪˈnæmɪks ɑ kʌnˈtɹoːʊld baːɪ bɹɛθ lɪˈgatoːʊ ænd ˈvaːɪbɹænsɪ (spɪn)]

[ˈtɛnʃʌn ɪnˈhɪbɪts ðʌ ˈsɪŋʌz ʌˈbɪlɪtɪ tu kʌnˈtɹoːʊl kɹɪˈʃɛndoːʊ]

[kɹɪˈʃɛndoːʊ ɪz ʌ daːɪægˈnastɪk tul – ɪt ˈɪndɪkɛːɪts ðʌ ˈlɛvʊl ʌv ˈfɹidʌm]

[ʌ ɾɪˈlist toːʊn hæz ðʌ ˈfɹidʌm tu gɹoːʊ æt ðʌ kʌˈmand ʌv ðʌ ˈsɪŋʌ]

[kɹɪˈʃɛndoːʊ ɾɪˈkwaːɪʌz]:

1. [ɹɪˈlis ʌv ˌɪntʌˈfiːʌɾɪŋ ˈmʌskjulʌ ˈtɛnʃʌn]

2. [kʌnˈtɪnjuʌs floːʊ ʌv ɛːʌ]

3. [vaːɪˈbɹatoːʊ]

Exercise

[sɪŋ ðʌ ˈfaloːʊɪŋ ˈɛksʌsaːɪz ʍaːɪl ˈsloːʊlɪ ˈtɜnɪŋ ðʌ hɛd "no"]

[mɛːɪnˈtɛːɪn vaːɪˈbɹatoːʊ baːɪ ɾɪˈlisɪŋ ˌɪntʌˈfiːʌɾɪŋ ˈtɛnʃʌn]

[ðʌ fɜst noːʊt ɪz ˈvɛɾɪ saft ænd ˈspɪnɪŋ]

[ɪt kʌˈnɛkts tu ði ˈʌpʌ toːʊnz ɪn æn ˌʌnɪntʌˈɾʌptɛd floːʊ ʌv saːʊnd]

[bɪˈgɪn ðʌ kɹɪˈʃɛndoːʊ an ði ˈʌpʌ ɛf ænd gɹoːʊ ðʌ spɪn ˈɪntu ðʌ skɛːɪl]

[du nat ɹʌʃ ði ˈɛksʌsaːɪz - ðʌ pɪtʃ muvz ʍɛn ˈvaːɪbɹænsɪ ɪz ˈaptɪmaːɪzd]

~ George Bitzas

Notes

Personal Assessment

Breath

Breath Control   70-------------79/80-------------89/90-------------100
Breath Expansion   70-------------79/80-------------89/90-------------100
Breath Support   70-------------79/80-------------89/90-------------100

Diction

Consonant Articulation 70-------------79/80-------------89/90-------------100
Vowel Formation   70-------------79/80-------------89/90-------------100

Musicianship

Expression   70-------------79/80-------------89/90-------------100
Legato   70-------------79/80-------------89/90-------------100
Pitch Accuracy   70-------------79/80-------------89/90-------------100
Rhythmic Accuracy   70-------------79/80-------------89/90-------------100

Posture and Tension

Postural Alignment   70-------------79/80-------------89/90-------------100
Release of Tension   70-------------79/80-------------89/90-------------100

Technique

Flexibility   70-------------79/80-------------89/90-------------100
Onset   70-------------79/80-------------89/90-------------100
Palatal Space   70-------------79/80-------------89/90-------------100
Pharyngeal Space   70-------------79/80-------------89/90-------------100
Projection   70-------------79/80-------------89/90-------------100
Vibrato   70-------------79/80-------------89/90-------------100
Tone Quality   70-------------79/80-------------89/90-------------100
Vowel Equalization   70-------------79/80-------------89/90-------------100

Stage Deportment

[stɛːɪʤ dɪˈpɔtmɛnt pɜˈtɛːɪnz tu ˈɛtɪkɛt fɔ ðʌ ˈkanˈsɜt stɛːɪʤ]

[ðɛːʌɾ ɑ sɪks kʌmˈpoːʊnɛnts ʌv stɛːɪʤ dɪˈpɔtmɛnt]:

1. [ʌˈtaːɪʌ – jɔːʌɾ ʌˈpɪːʌræns ʌˈfɛkts haːʊ ju ɑ pɜˈsivd baːɪ ði ˈɔdɪɛns]

[ʌˈtaːɪʌɾ ɪz ˈvɛɾɪ ɪmˈpɔtænt ɪn ðʌ pɜˈfɔmɪŋ ɑts]

2. [ˈɛntɹæns – wɔk an stɛːɪʤ wɪð ˈkanfɪdɛns ænd ˈpɜpʌs]

[mɛːɪnˈtɛːɪn ʌ ˈplɛzænt ɪkˈspɹɛʃʌn æz ju gɹit jɔːʌ ˈɔdɪɛns]

3. [ˈbaːʊɪŋ – ˈbaːʊɪŋ ɪz æn ɪkˈspɹɛʃʌn ʌv ˈgɹætɪtjud fɔ ʌˈplɔz]

[ðʌ baːʊ ɪz lɛs dip fɔ ði ˈɛntɹæns baːʊ]

[ðʌ baːʊ æt ði ɛnd ʌv ʌ pɜˈfɔmæns ɪz ˈdipʌɾ ænd hɛld ʌ ˈlɪtʊl ˈlaŋgʌ]

[bɛnd æt ðʌ wɛːɪst ænd baːʊ wɪð ði ɪnˈtaːɪʌ tɹʌŋk ʌv ðʌ ˈbadɪ ænd hɛd]

4. [pɜˈfɔmɪŋ – kip ˈʤɛsʧʊz ˈʤɛnjuɪn ænd ˈgɹɛːɪsfʊl]

[ʌˈvɔːɪd ˈfɛːɪʃʊl ɪkˈspɹɛʃʌnz ðæt kʌmˈjunɪkɛːɪt ˈnɛgʌtɪv ɪˈmoːʊʃʌnz]

[ænd du nat lɛt ˈɛɾɔz ʃoːʊ an jɔːʌ fɛːɪs – kip ɪt ˈpazɪtɪv]

5. [spiʧ – pɹɪˈpɛːʌ jɔːʌ wɜdz ˈkɛːʌfʊlɪ]

[pɹoˈnaːʊns wɪð ˈækjʊɾæsɪ ænd ʌˈvɔːɪd gɹʌˈmætɪkʊl ˈɛɾɔz] *Sample:*

[ˈmɪstʌ ˈɔstɪn ænd aːɪ wɪl bi pɜˈfɔmɪŋ ɔr ke il ʧɛlo baːɪ vɪnˈʧɛntso ɾiˈgini]

6. [ækˈnalɛʤmɛnts – tɛːɪk ʌ baːʊ ˈfaloːʊɪŋ ði ʌˈplɔz]

[ðɛn ækˈnalɛʤ jɔːʌɾ ʌˈkʌmpænɪst ænd baːʊ tuˈgɛðʌ]

Notes

Personal Assessment

Breath

Breath Control	70	79/80	89/90	100
Breath Expansion	70	79/80	89/90	100
Breath Support	70	79/80	89/90	100

Diction

Consonant Articulation	70	79/80	89/90	100
Vowel Formation	70	79/80	89/90	100

Musicianship

Expression	70	79/80	89/90	100
Legato	70	79/80	89/90	100
Pitch Accuracy	70	79/80	89/90	100
Rhythmic Accuracy	70	79/80	89/90	100

Posture and Tension

Postural Alignment	70	79/80	89/90	100
Release of Tension	70	79/80	89/90	100

Technique

Flexibility	70	79/80	89/90	100
Onset	70	79/80	89/90	100
Palatal Space	70	79/80	89/90	100
Pharyngeal Space	70	79/80	89/90	100
Projection	70	79/80	89/90	100
Vibrato	70	79/80	89/90	100
Tone Quality	70	79/80	89/90	100
Vowel Equalization	70	79/80	89/90	100

Vocal Health

[jɔːʌ ˈbadɪ ɪz jɔːʌ ˈɪnstrumɛnt tɛːɪk kɛːʌr ʌv jɔːʌ ˈbadɪ]

1. [ðʌ vɔːɪs ɹɪˈkwɑːɪʌz hɑːɪˈdɹɛːɪʃʌn – dɹɪŋk ˈplɛntɪ ʌv ˈwɔtʌ]

2. [kæˈfin ænd ˈælkʌˌhal dɪˈplit ðʌ ˈsɪstʌm ʌv ˈwɔtʌ – ˈlɪmɪt jus]

3. [ʌˈvɔːɪd ˈsmoːʊkɪŋ (ðɪs ɪnˈkludz ˈsɛkʌnd hænd smoːʊk)]

4. [kɛːʌ fɔ jɔːʌ ˈdʒɛnʌrʊl hɛlθ (ɹɛst ˈɛksʌsɑːɪz ænd ˈdɑːɪɛt)]

5. [kɛːʌ fɔ jɔːʌ ˈɪnʌ hɛlθ (ˈspɪrɪt ænd mɑːɪnd)]

6. [ʌˈvɔːɪd θroːʊt ˈklɪːʌrɪŋ ænd haʃ ˈkɔfɪŋ]

7. [ˈlɪmɪt ðʌ jus ʌv jɔːʌ vɔːɪs ɪn ˈnɔːɪzɪ ɪnˈvɑːɪrʌnmɛnts]

Sick Day

[doːʊnt sɪŋ ɪf jɔːʌ θroːʊt ɪz sɔːʌ]

[ju kæn sɪŋ wɪð ʌ koːʊld æz laŋ æz ðɛːʌr ɪz noːʊ dɪsˈkʌmfɔt ɪn ðʌ θroːʊt]

[ˈθɔtfʊl ˈmjuzɪkʊl pɹɛpaˈrɛːɪʃʌnz kæn kʌnˈtɪnju (hɛlθ pɜˈmɪtɪŋ)]

[hɪːʌr ɑ lɪŋks tu ˈɹɪsɔsɛz fɔ vɔːɪs ɹɪˈlɛːɪtɛd ˈstʌdɪ ænd pɹɛpaˈrɛːɪʃʌn]:

Art songs with translation: http://www.lieder.net/

Art songs with IPA: www.ipasource.com

Listening lab: http://www.stmpublishers.com/listening.html

Dictionary: https://en.pons.com/translate

IPA Scramble (free app): https://itunes.apple.com/us/app/ipa-scramble/id1165103246?mt=8 (or stmpublishers.com)

Articulatory Phonetics: Week 11

Day 1: Vowel Terms

Day 2: Consonant Terms

Day 3: Vowel Quiz

Day 4: Consonant Quiz

Day 5: Singing Quiz – Vowels

Day 6: Singing Quiz – Consonants

Lesson Notes, Date: _____________

Checklist of Concepts to Review

BREATH
Breath Control___
p: 35, 63, 67
Breath Support___
p: 63, 65
Breath Expansion___
p: 33, 35
DICTION
Articulation___
p: 121, 123, 125, 131
Front Vowels___
p: 57, 105
Back Vowels___
p: 73, 107
Central Vowels___
p: 89, 91, 93, 109, 111
Mixed Vowels___
p: 113, 115
FLEXIBILITY
Flexibility___
p: 109, 139
MUSICIANSHIP
Artistry___
p: 141
Dynamics___
p: 143
Legato___
p: 49, 59, 75, 139, 141

POSTURE
Postural Alignment___
p: 25, 27
RANGE
Range___
p: 81, 91, 139
TONE
Chiaroscuro___
p: 97, 113, 115
Lip Trills___
p: 41, 43
Palatal Resonance___
p: 89, 91, 93, 109
Pharyngeal Space___
p: 57, 59, 93, 105, 109
Projection___
p: 73, 75, 93, 107
Register___
p: 43, 83
Resonance___
p: 93, 95, 97, 109, 137
Sensory Awareness___
p: 61, 127
Vibrato___
p: 43, 45, 51, 77, 79, 81
Vowel Equalization___
p: 79, 95, 137
WARM-UPS___
p: 200-204

WARNINGS
Breathy Tone___
p: 35, 77, 113, 125, 127
Faulty Formation___
p. 111, 127
Faulty Movement___
p. 45, 47
Faulty Onset___
p: 59, 75, 127
Jaw Tension___
p: 31, 111, 121, 123, 125
Nasal Tone ___
p: 111, 127
Pressed Tone___
p: 35, 41, 43, 83
Spread Tone___
p: 57, 61, 73, 111
Tension___
p: 29, 31, 45, 47, 61
Tongue Impeded Tone__
p: 111, 127
OTHER
Choral Singing___
p: 99
Stage Deportment___
p: 145
Vocal health___
p: 147

Daily Notes and Practice Times

Day 1 Practice Time:______________

Day 2 Practice Time:______________

Day 3 Practice Time:______________

Day 4 Practice Time:______________

Day 5 Practice Time:______________

Day 6 Practice Time:______________

Vowel Terms

FRONT VOWELS are also called tongue vowels. They require a front arch of the tongue. There are two fundamental closed front vowels: [i] and [e]. Each has a corresponding open vowel form:
closed [i] *see* < open [ɪ] *bit*
closed [e] *chaos* < open [ɛ] *said*

BACK VOWELS are also called lip vowels. They require lip rounding and a back tongue arch. There are two fundamental closed back vowels: [u] and [o]. Each has a corresponding open vowel form:
closed [u] *blue* < open [ʊ] *look*
closed [o] *provide* < open [ɔ] *ought*

MIXED VOWELS require lip rounding and a front tongue arch. There are two fundamental closed vowels with a corresponding open vowel form:
[i] tongue + [u] lip = closed [y] *früh, une*
[ɪ] tongue + [ʊ] lip = open [ʏ] *Glück*
[e] tongue + [o] lip = closed [ø] *schön, yeux*
[ɛ] tongue + [ɔ] lip = open [œ] *möcht, cœur*

CENTRAL VOWELS do not require lip rounding. There are four central vowels: dark [ɑ] *father*, bright [a] *voila*, [æ] *hat*, [ʌ] *up*
The [ɒ] vowel, as in *hot*, is between [ɑ] and [ɔ] (not used in this text).

There are two *r* colored vowels: English [ɜ] *bird*, and German [ʁ] *der*. The [ɝ], [ɚ], and [ɐ] vowel *r* symbols represent speech formation and are not suitable for lyric diction since they merge the *r* with a schwa.

NASAL VOWELS resonate in the height of the yawn space with a small amount of shared resonant space in the nasal cavity. There are four nasal vowels: [ã], [ɛ̃], [õ], and [œ̃]

THE SCHWA [ə] is an undefined vowel sound in an unstressed syllable. Pronunciation must be assigned for each language.

The Singer's Mouth. An adjustment is made to accommodate the space needed for singing. The jaw should remain released for all vowels. Formation is created with the tongue for tongue vowels, with the lips for lip vowels, and by clarifying the resonance for central vowels. The tongue tip must always contact the lower row of front teeth (except [ɜ]) and the lips must never spread as they do in speech. Closed and open designations refer to space between the palate and tongue arch – the tongue arch is closer to the palate for closed vowels.

Consonant Terms

VOICING refers to vocal engagement. A voiced consonant engages the vocal cords. A voiceless consonant employs air alone.

POINT OF ARTICULATION refers to the point of contact between the lips, teeth, tongue, palate, and glottis.
Bilabial. Refers to the lips: [m], [b], [p], [w], English [ʍ]
Labiodental. Involves the lower lip and upper row of teeth: [v], [f]
Dental. Involves the tip of the tongue and the back of the upper row of teeth: English [ð] and [θ], Italian and French [d], [n], [t], [l], [z], [s], [r], Italian [r], German [l], [z], and [s]
Alveolar. Involves the tongue tip and the ridge behind the upper teeth: English [d], [n], [t], [l], [z], [s], [r], [ɹ], German [d], [n], [t], [r]
Prepalatal. Involves the tip of tongue and the area between the alveolar ridge and hard palate: [ʃ], Italian and French [j], English and French [ʒ], English, Italian, and German [tʃ], French [ɲ] and [ɥ], Italian [ɲ] and [ʎ], and English and Italian [dʒ]
Palatal. Involves a front arch of the tongue and the hard palate: English and German [j], German ich-Laut [ç]
Velar. Involves a back arch of the tongue and the soft palate: [g] and [k], German ach-Laut [x], English, Italian, and German [ŋ]
Glottal. Involves the air flow and the opening between the vocal cords: English and German [ʔ] and [h]

MANNER OF ARTICULATION refers to air flow.
Stop. A momentary closure of the air flow: [b], [d], [g], [p], [t], [k], [ʔ]
Plosive. A momentary closure of the air flow passage that releases without aspiration: Italian and French [b], [d], [g], [p], [t], [k]
Fricative. Produced by directing the air flow past a set of articulators: [ʍ], [v], [f], [ð], [θ], [z], [s], [ʒ], [ʃ], [ç], [x], and [h]
Affricate. A stop followed by a fricative: [dz], [ts], [dʒ], [tʃ], [pf]
Nasal. Produced by directing vocalized tone through the nasal passages: [m], [n], [ɲ], [ŋ]
Lateral. Produced by directing vocalized tone laterally over the sides of the tongue: [l] and [ʎ]
Glide. Produced by directing vocalized tone past a set of articulators without friction: [w], [j], and [ɥ] (also classified as semivowels)
Trill. Formed by taps with the tip of the tongue against the alveolar ridge or upper front teeth: rolled [r] and flipped [ɾ]
Retroflex. Produced with tongue tip curled up: English [ɹ]

Vowel Quiz

1. List the front vowels and their corresponding open vowel form:

2. List the back vowels and their corresponding open vowel form:

3. List the mixed vowels and their corresponding open vowel form:

4. List the central vowels:

5. List the nasal vowels:

6. What is the schwa?

See page 152 for the answers.

Consonant Quiz

1. Provide the voiceless counterpart for the following consonants:

      [b]   [v]

      [d]   [z]

      [g]   [ð]

      [w]   [ʤ]

      [ʒ]

2. List the consonant points of articulation:

3. Provide the manner of articulation for the following:

    [b], [d], [g], [p], [t], [k], [ʔ] ＿＿＿＿＿＿＿＿

    [z], [s], [ʒ], [ʃ], [ç], [x], [h] ＿＿＿＿＿＿＿

    [dz], [ts], [dʒ], [tʃ], [pf] ＿＿＿＿＿＿＿＿

    [m], [n], [ɲ], [ŋ]＿＿＿＿＿＿＿＿＿＿

    [ʍ], [v], [f], [ð], [θ]＿＿＿＿＿＿＿＿

    [l], [ʎ]＿＿＿＿＿＿＿＿＿＿＿＿＿

    [w], [j], [ɥ]＿＿＿＿＿＿＿＿＿＿＿

    [r], [ɾ]＿＿＿＿＿＿＿＿＿＿＿＿＿＿

    [ɹ]＿＿＿＿＿＿＿＿＿＿＿＿＿＿＿＿

See page 153 for the answers.

Singing Quiz – Vowels

Sing the following:

1. Sing a descending slide on each of the following vowels:

    [i] [ɪ] [e] [ɛ] [u] [ʊ] [o] [ɔ] [a] [ɑ] [y] [ʏ] [ø] [œ]

2. Sing a descending scale on each of the following vowels:

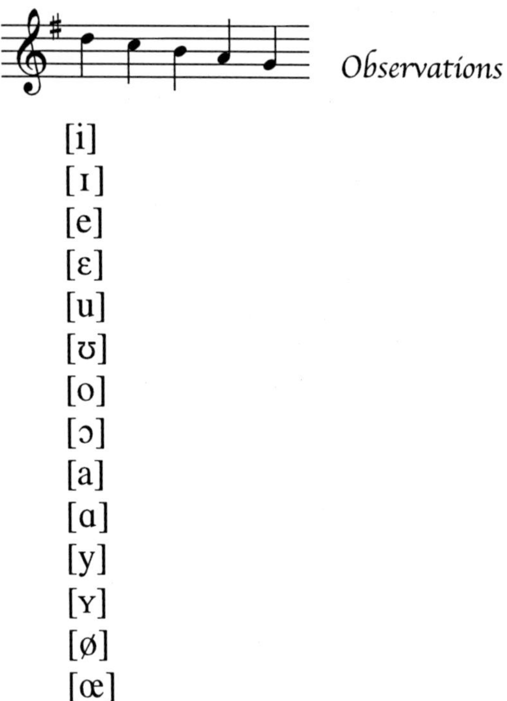

[i]
[ɪ]
[e]
[ɛ]
[u]
[ʊ]
[o]
[ɔ]
[a]
[ɑ]
[y]
[ʏ]
[ø]
[œ]

3. Choose one of the following vowel sequences and sing it on one note:

    [i e a o u]

    [u i e a o u]

    [a i e a o u]

Singing Quiz – Consonants

1. Sing the following:

Goals:

To maintain vowel space and establish an uninterrupted vowel chain
To articulate in a rapid, late, and clear manner ~ *Thomas Grubb*

2. Sing the following sequence on one note. Observe the breath marks:
[aːp ✓ aːt ✓ aːk ✓ aːʃ ✓ aːf ✓ aːx]

Goal:

To fully aspirate final consonants

3. Sing the following sequence on one note. Observe the breath marks:
[aːb ✓ aːd ✓ aːg]

Goal:

To fully voice the final consonants by adding a schwa

4. Sing the following sequence on one note. Observe the breath marks:
[aːv ✓ aːz ✓ aːm ✓ aːn ✓ aːŋ ✓ aːl ✓ iːl]

Goal:

To fully voice final consonants without adding a schwa

Italian Pronunciation Guide

IPA	English	Italian	Italian Formation
[i]	see [si]	ivi ['ivi]	the tongue arch is far forward; more forward than in English
[e]	chaos ['keɑs]	perché [per'ke]	between the [i] and [ɛ] vowel; not a diphthong as in English
[ɛ]	bell [bɛl]	bene ['bɛne]	more forward than in English
[u]	dew [dju]	luna ['luna]	forward lip rounding; more rounded than in English
[o]	obey [ʔo'bɛɪ]	solo ['solo]	forward lip rounding; not a diphthong as in English
[ɔ]	ought [ʔɔt]	core ['kɔɾe]	forward lip rounding initiated by the cheek muscles
[a]	sigh (Am) [sai]	cara ['kaɾa]	brighter quality than in English; not a diphthong
[ɾ]	thread [θɾɛd]	parola [pa'ɾola]	one flip of the tongue tip against the upper front teeth
[r]		rosa ['rɔza]	articulate a fully voiced rolled "r" with the tongue tip
[ʃ]	shoe [ʃu]	lascia ['laʃʃa]	elongate the Italian [ʃʃ]
[tʃ]	child [tʃaɪld]	cielo ['tʃɛlo]	articulate two voiceless consonants
[dʒ]	judge [dʒʌdʒ]	gioia ['dʒɔja]	articulate two voiced consonants
[ɲ]		sogno ['soɲɲo]	[j] tongue position with a nasal manner of articulation
[ʎ]		figlio ['fiʎʎo]	[j] tongue with a lateral air flow; articulate [l] with tongue tip down
[j]	young [jʌŋ]	miei [mjɛːi]	a rapidly enunciated [i]
[ŋ]	wing [wɪŋ]	lungo ['luŋgo]	[g] tongue position with a nasal manner of articulation
[d][n][t][l]	dental ['dɛntəl]	dentale [den'tale]	the tongue tip contacts the upper front teeth in Italian
[b][d][g]	bag [bæg]	albergo [al'bɛrgo]	fully voice without aspiration in Italian
[p][t][k]	kept [kɛpt]	scolpito [skɔl'pito]	articulate without aspiration in Italian

Italian Diction: Week 12

Day 1: Introduction to Italian Diction

Day 2: Italian [i] and [a]

Day 3: Italian [e] and [ɛ]

Day 4: Italian [u] and Double Consonants

Day 5: Italian [o] and [ɔ]

Day 6: Italian Double Consonants – Stops

Lesson Notes, Date: ___________

Checklist of Concepts to Review

BREATH
Breath Control___
p: 35, 63, 67
Breath Support___
p: 63, 65
Breath Expansion___
p: 33, 35
DICTION
Articulation___
p: 121, 123, 125, 131
Front Vowels___
p: 57, 105
Back Vowels___
p: 73, 107
Central Vowels___
p: 89, 91, 93, 109, 111
Mixed Vowels___
p: 113, 115
FLEXIBILITY
Flexibility___
p: 109, 139
MUSICIANSHIP
Artistry___
p: 141
Dynamics___
p: 143
Legato___
p: 49, 59, 75, 139, 141

POSTURE
Postural Alignment___
p: 25, 27
RANGE
Range___
p: 81, 91, 139
TONE
Chiaroscuro___
p: 97, 113, 115
Lip Trills___
p: 41, 43
Palatal Resonance___
p: 89, 91, 93, 109
Pharyngeal Space___
p: 57, 59, 93, 105, 109
Projection___
p: 73, 75, 93, 107
Register___
p: 43, 83
Resonance___
p: 93, 95, 97, 109, 137
Sensory Awareness___
p: 61, 127
Vibrato___
p: 43, 45, 51, 77, 79, 81
Vowel Equalization___
p: 79, 95, 137
WARM-UPS___
p: 200-204

WARNINGS
Breathy Tone___
p: 35, 77, 113, 125, 127
Faulty Formation___
p. 111, 127
Faulty Movement___
p. 45, 47
Faulty Onset___
p: 59, 75, 127
Jaw Tension___
p: 31, 111, 121, 123, 125
Nasal Tone ___
p: 111, 127
Pressed Tone___
p: 35, 41, 43, 83
Spread Tone___
p: 57, 61, 73, 111
Tension___
p: 29, 31, 45, 47, 61
Tongue Impeded Tone__
p: 111, 127
OTHER
Choral Singing___
p: 99
Stage Deportment___
p: 145
Vocal health___
p: 147

Daily Notes and Practice Times

Day 1   Practice Time:___________

Day 2   Practice Time:___________

Day 3   Practice Time:___________

Day 4   Practice Time:___________

Day 5   Practice Time:___________

Day 6   Practice Time:___________

Introduction to Italian Diction

Attributes of the language. Italian vowels sound "excessively neat and strong and precise" to the English speaker's ear (Colorni, p. 13). The front vowel tongue arch is more forward and the back vowel lip formation is more rounded than the English formation of the same symbols. English vowels are medial in placement while the Italian vowels are described as resonating "in the mask" (*Great Singers on Singing*, by Jerome Hines, p. 293).

The structure of the Italian language is ideal for singing. The lyrical flow of words enhances the singer's ability to focus on the vowels. Proper formation of Italian vowels and an energized articulation of the consonants lead to beautiful singing (*bel canto*).

Stress in Italian. Stress is not formed by a weighted accentuation as in English. The pitch rises and then slides down during an elongation of the vowel sound. Stress in Italian is produced by lengthening the vowel.

Vowels. Italian vowels are devoid of any on or off-glide of the sound. Vowel clarity is not weakened in unstressed syllables. Avoid the medial placement of English vowels and do not diphthongize the Italian monophthongs. The glottal stop does not exist in Italian.

Dental consonants. The consonants in the word *dental* are articulated with the tongue tip touching the upper front teeth. Dental consonants have no aspiration in the tone. Contrast the following English/Italian words: *decide/decidere* [de'tʃidere] *table/tavolo* ['tavolo]

Plosive consonants. Voiced *b, d, g,* and their voiceless counterparts *p, t, k,* are articulated with no aspiration in the tone. Contrast the following English/Italian words: *baby/bambino* [bam'bino] *pure/pure* ['pure]

IPA symbols. The phonetic symbols needed for Italian lyric diction are defined on page 158. A free diction listening lab is available on the listening page at www.stmpublishers.com.

Assignment: Record the word lists in the following lessons.

Italian [i] and [a]

Highlighted Sounds	#1	#2
[n] [i] [a]	mani/hands ['mani]	vini/wines ['vini]
[t] [i] [a]	vita/life ['vita]	imiti/you imitate ['imiti]
[s] [z] [i] [a]	stami/yarns ['stami]	sì/yes [si]
[l] [i] [a]	fili/threads ['fili]	alfin/at last [al'fin]
[d] [i] [a]	indi/therefore ['indi]	dita/fingers ['dita]
[ɾ]	dirà/he will say [di'ɾa]	mira/he aims ['miɾa]
[k] [i] [a]	antica/ancient [an'tika]	cari/dears ['kaɾi]
[p] [i] [a]	palpiti/heart beats ['palpiti]	tapini/miserable [ta'pini]
[g] [i] [a]	vaghi/vague ['vagi]	aghi/needles ['agi]
[b] [i] [a]	banditi/bandits [ban'diti]	bambina/little girl [bam'bina]
Initial [r]	riva/shore ['riva]	ridi/you laugh ['ridi]
Final [r]	marinar/sailor [maɾi'nar]	spasimar/to be smitten [spazi'mar]
Medial [r]	gradita/appreciated [gra'dita]	partir/to leave [par'tir]
[iː]	sia/it may be [siːa]	mia/mine [miːa]
[aː]	hai/you have [aːi]	vai/you go [vaːi]

Italian [e] and [ɛ]

Highlighted Sounds	#1	#2
[e]	le/the [le]	re/king [re]
[e] [e]	perché/because [perˈke]	crede/he believes [ˈkrede]
[i] [e]	rime/rhymes [ˈrime]	vile/base [ˈvile]
[a] [e]	spirate/died [spiˈrate]	libertà/freedom [liberˈta]
[ɛ]	bel/beautiful [bɛl]	ben/well [bɛn]
[ɛ] [e]	feste/festivities [ˈfɛste]	sempre/always [ˈsɛmpre]
[ɛ] [i]	sensi/senses [ˈsɛnsi]	preghi/pleadings [ˈprɛgi]
[ɛ] [a]	destra/right [ˈdɛstra]	ardenti/burning [arˈdɛnti]
[i] [e] [ɛ] [a]	inesperta/inexperienced [inesˈpɛrta]	deserti/deserts [deˈzɛrti]
[j]	chiama/he calls [ˈkjama]	pianti/cries [ˈpjanti]
[eː] [ɛː]	nei/in the [neːi]	scriverei/I would write [skriveˈrɛːi]
[tʃ]	dice/says [ˈditʃe]	mercè/mercy [merˈtʃe]
[dʒ]	agili/agile [ˈadʒili]	gente/people [ˈdʒɛnte]
[ŋ]	tenga/he may hold [ˈtɛŋga]	franca/open [ˈfraŋka]

Italian [u] and Double Consonants

Highlighted Sounds	#1	#2
[u]	d'un/of a [dʊn]	giù/down [dʒu]
[u] [e]	pure/too [ˈpuɾe]	lunghe/long [ˈluŋge]
[u] [i]	venuti/come [veˈnuti]	ultimi/last [ˈultimi]
[u] [a]	usanza/custom [uˈzantsa]	fugace/fleeting [fuˈgatʃe]
[j] [u]	liuta/lute [ˈljuta]	giustizia/justice [dʒusˈtitsja]
[uː]	fui/I was [fuːi]	sue/its [suːe]
[aː]	inaudita/unheard of [inaːuˈdita]	gaudi/joys [ˈgaːudi]
[nn]	canna/pipe [ˈkanna]	penna/feather [ˈpenna]
[mm]	immagine/image [imˈmadʒine]	dramma/drama [ˈdramma]
[ll]	stelle/stars [ˈstelle]	capelli/hair [kaˈpelli]
[rr]	arranca/it hobbles [arˈraŋka]	verrà/it will come [verˈra]
[ɲɲ]	lagna/whine [ˈlaɲɲa]	bagni/baths [ˈbaɲɲi]
[ʎʎ]	dagli/from the [ˈdaʎʎi]	agli/to the [ˈaʎʎi]
[z]	snella/slender [ˈznɛlla]	svaniti/vanished [zvaˈniti]

Italian [o] and [ɔ]

Highlighted Sounds	#1	#2
[u] final [o]	giusto/just [ˈdʒusto]	crudo/raw [ˈkɾudo]
[o] final [o]	volto/face [ˈvolto]	sogno/dream [ˈsoɲɲo]
[o] [u] [i] [a]	fortuna/fortune [forˈtuna]	l'ultimo/the last [ˈlultimo]
[o] final [e]	onde/waves [ˈonde]	voce/voice [ˈvotʃe]
3 Syllables Final [e]	splendore/splendor [splenˈdoɾe]	odiare/to hate [oˈdjaɾe]
[o/u/a/i/e/ɛ]	cherubino/cherubim [keɾuˈbino]	adulatore/flatterer [adulaˈtoɾe]
3 Syllables Final [o]	profondo/depth [proˈfondo]	misero/wretched [ˈmizeɾo]
4-5 Syllables Final [o]	tradimento/treason [tradiˈmento]	dimenticato/forgotten [dimentiˈkato]
4-5 Syllables Final [e]	dimorare/to reside [dimoˈɾaɾe]	traditore/traitor [tradiˈtoɾe]
[ɔ]	forza/force [ˈfɔrtsa]	nobile/noble [ˈnɔbile]
[ɔ] [o]	poco/little [ˈpɔko]	bosco/forest [ˈbɔsko]
Challenge words [ɔ]	riposo/rest [riˈpɔzo]	insolito/unusual [inˈsɔlito]
[w]	qualche/some [ˈkwalke]	sguardo/look [ˈzgwardo]
[oː] [ɔːi]	vuoi/you want [vwɔːi]	ohimè/oh dear [oːiˈmɛ]
[iːo] [ɛːo]	addio/goodbye [adˈdiːo]	mio/mine [miːo]

Italian Double Consonants – Stops

Highlighted Sounds	#1	#2
[pp]	appare/it appears [apˈpaɾe]	doppio/double [ˈdoppjo]
[bb]	debbo/I must [ˈdɛbbo]	abbandonata/abandoned [abbandoˈnata]
[tt]	notte/night [ˈnɔtte]	letto/bed [ˈlɛtto]
[dd]	freddura/pun [fredˈduɾa]	raddolcire/to sweeten [raddolˈtʃiɾe]
[kk]	specchio/mirror [ˈspɛkkjo]	bocca/mouth [ˈbokka]
[gg]	traggo/I pull [ˈtraggo]	mugghiando/roaring [mugˈgjando]
[ttʃ]	riccioli/curls [ˈrittʃoli]	faccia/face [ˈfattʃa]
[ddʒ]	gregge/flock [ˈgreddʒe]	soggiorno/stay [sodˈdʒorno]
[tts] [ddz]	carezze/caresses [kaˈɾettse]	brezza/breeze [ˈbreddza]
[ʃʃ]	l'uscio/the door [ˈluʃʃo]	pesce/fish [ˈpeʃʃe]
[ff]	zeffiri/zephyrs [ˈdzɛffiɾi]	offese/offenses [ofˈfeze]
[ss]	spesso/often [ˈspesso]	lasso/tired [ˈlasso]
Challenge words	fiammella/flame [fjamˈmɛlla]	agnelli/lambs [aɲˈɲɛlli]
Challenge words	oppresso/oppressed [opˈprɛsso]	passeggero/passenger [passedˈdʒɛɾo]
Double stops	accetto/I accept [atˈtʃɛtto]	mezzanotte/midnight [meddzaˈnɔtte]

German Pronunciation Guide

IPA	English	German	German Formation
[i]	see [si]	Lied [li:t]	the tongue arch is far forward; more forward than in English
[ɪ]	wit [wɪt]	Bitte [ˈbɪttə]	placement is more forward than in English
[e]	chaos [ˈkeɑs]	Erde [ˈʔe:ɾdə]	between the [i] and [ɛ] vowel; not a diphthong as in English
[ɛ]	bell [bɛl]	Feld [fɛlt]	placement is more forward than in English
[u]	dew [dju]	Ruhe [ˈɾu:ə]	forward lip rounding; more rounded than in English
[ʊ]	look [lʊk]	jung [jʊŋ]	forward lip rounding; more rounded than in English
[o]	obey [ʔoˈbɛɪ]	Mond [mo:nt]	forward lip rounding; not a diphthong as in English
[ɔ]	ought [ʔɔt]	Sonne [ˈzɔnnə]	forward lip rounding initiated by the cheek muscles
[a]	sigh (Am) [sai]	allein [ʔalˈlaen]	brighter quality than in English; not a diphthong
[ɑ]	father [ˈfɑðə]	Abend [ˈʔɑ:bənt]	similar to English [ɑ]
[y]		Blüte [ˈbly:tə]	[i] tongue arch with [u] lip rounding
[ʏ]		Küsse [ˈkʏssə]	[ɪ] tongue arch with [ʊ] lip rounding
[ø]		schön [ʃø:n]	[e] tongue arch, [o] lip rounding, and color of [ɜ]
[œ]		können [ˈkœnnən]	[ɛ] tongue arch with [ɔ] lip rounding
[ʁ]		Vater [ˈfɑ:təʁ]	pronounce an American "r" with the tongue tip down
[ɾ]	thread [θɾɛd]	rot [ɾo:t]	one flip of the tongue tip against the upper front teeth
[ʃ]	shoe [ʃu]	Sterne [ˈʃtɛɾnə]	voiceless sibilant
[tʃ]	child [tʃaɪld]	Deutsch [dɔøtʃ]	articulate two voiceless consonants
[ç]	huge [çjudʒ]	Licht [lɪçt]	[i] tongue arch with aspirated articulation; air flows through a constricted passage
[j]	young [jʌŋ]	Jahr [jɑ:ɾ]	a rapidly enunciated [i]
[ŋ]	wing [wɪŋ]	Engel [ˈʔɛŋəl]	[g] tongue position with a nasal manner of articulation
[x]		Nacht [naxt]	[u] tongue arch with aspirated articulation; air flows through a constricted passage

German Diction: Week 13

Day 1: Introduction to German Diction

Day 2: Closed Vowels and Dark [ɑ]

Day 3: Open Vowels and Bright [a]

Day 4: Double Consonants

Day 5: Mixed Vowels

Day 6: Diphthongs, Ich-Laut, Ach-Laut

Lesson Notes, Date: _____________

Checklist of Concepts to Review

BREATH
Breath Control___
p: 35, 63, 67
Breath Support___
p: 63, 65
Breath Expansion___
p: 33, 35
DICTION
Articulation___
p: 121, 123, 125, 131
Front Vowels___
p: 57, 105
Back Vowels___
p: 73, 107
Central Vowels___
p: 89, 91, 93, 109, 111
Mixed Vowels___
p: 113, 115
FLEXIBILITY
Flexibility___
p: 109, 139
MUSICIANSHIP
Artistry___
p: 141
Dynamics___
p: 143
Legato___
p: 49, 59, 75, 139, 141

POSTURE
Postural Alignment___
p: 25, 27
RANGE
Range___
p: 81, 91, 139
TONE
Chiaroscuro___
p: 97, 113, 115
Lip Trills___
p: 41, 43
Palatal Resonance___
p: 89, 91, 93, 109
Pharyngeal Space___
p: 57, 59, 93, 105, 109
Projection___
p: 73, 75, 93, 107
Register___
p: 43, 83
Resonance___
p: 93, 95, 97, 109, 137
Sensory Awareness___
p: 61, 127
Vibrato___
p: 43, 45, 51, 77, 79, 81
Vowel Equalization___
p: 79, 95, 137
WARM-UPS___
p: 200-204

WARNINGS
Breathy Tone___
p: 35, 77, 113, 125, 127
Faulty Formation___
p. 111, 127
Faulty Movement___
p. 45, 47
Faulty Onset___
p: 59, 75, 127
Jaw Tension___
p: 31, 111, 121, 123, 125
Nasal Tone ___
p: 111, 127
Pressed Tone___
p: 35, 41, 43, 83
Spread Tone___
p: 57, 61, 73, 111
Tension___
p: 29, 31, 45, 47, 61
Tongue Impeded Tone___
p: 111, 127
OTHER
Choral Singing___
p: 99
Stage Deportment___
p: 145
Vocal health___
p: 147

Daily Notes and Practice Times

Day 1 Practice Time:__________

Day 2 Practice Time:__________

Day 3 Practice Time:__________

Day 4 Practice Time:__________

Day 5 Practice Time:__________

Day 6 Practice Time:__________

Introduction to German Diction

Attributes of the language. German words contain a broad array of colorful vowels and a predominate occurrence of consonants clusters. These characteristics allow composers and singers to explore a wealth of musical expression. The German language is highly descriptive in nature having words that express ideas with intricate detail.

Intoning German lyric texts trains the singer to articulate consonants without losing the tall space needed for vowels.

Stress in German. The stressed syllable is characterized by a weighted accentuation. The vowel of the stressed syllable may be either long or short. The pitch is typically higher in the first syllable regardless of stress. As a general rule, polysyllabic words are stressed in the first syllable. Numerous exceptions apply.

Vowels. German vowels are forward in resonance. Avoid the medial placement of English vowels. German words typically contain one vowel per syllable. Do not diphthongize the German monophthongs.

Dental consonants. Spelling *l* and the consonants [s] and [z] are the only dental consonants in German. Avoid the Italian and French dental articulation of *d, n,* and *t.* These consonants are articulated with an alveolar point of contact in both English and German.

Voiceless aspirate consonants. Consonants *p, t, k,* are articulated with aspiration in German and English. Avoid the Italian and French non-aspirate articulation of the German stops.

IPA symbols. The phonetic symbols needed for German lyric diction are defined on page 168. A free diction listening lab is available on the listening page at www.stmpublishers.com.

Assignment: Record the word lists in the following lessons.

Closed Vowels and Dark [ɑ]

Highlighted Sounds	#1	#2
[iː]	tief/deep [tiːf]	sie/she [ziː]
[iː] [ə]	sieben/seven [ˈziːbən]	Biene/bee [ˈbiːnə]
[eː]	Klee/clover [kleː]	wem/whom [veːm]
[eː] [ə]	wehen/to blow [ˈveːən]	eben/even [ˈʔeːbən]
[uː]	du/you [duː]	tut/do [tuːt]
[uː] [ə]	Mute/cheer [ˈmuːtə]	Gluten/heat [ˈgluːtən]
[oː]	Hof/yard [hoːf]	Dom/cathedral [doːm]
[oː] [ə]	oben/above [ˈʔoːbən]	wohnen/live [ˈvoːnən]
[ɑː]	Zahl/number [tsɑːl]	Pfad/path [pfɑːt]
[ɑː] [ə]	Saaten/grains [ˈzɑːtən]	Knabe/boy [ˈknɑːbə]
Medial [ɾ]	Ehre/honor [ˈʔeːɾə]	Brief/letter [bɾiːf]
Intial/final [ɾ]	Riegel/latch [ˈɾiːgəl]	zur/to [tsuːɾ]
Vowel [ʁ]	der/the [deːʁ]	oder/or [ˈʔoːdəʁ]
Final [p]	Lob/praise [loːp]	gib/give [giːp]
Final [k]/[t]	Grad/grade [gɾɑːt]	Tag/day [tɑːk]
Challenge words	Natur/nature [nɑˈtuːɾ]	Poesie/poetry [poeˈziː]

Open Vowels and Bright [a]

Highlighted Sounds	#1	#2
[ɪ]	bist/are [bɪst]	im/in [ʔɪm]
[ɪ] [ə]	Linde/lime tree [ˈlɪndə]	finster/dark [ˈfɪnstəʁ]
Challenge words	Silberkieseln/silver pebbles [ˈzɪlbəʁkiːzəln]	Liebesblick/loving look [ˈliːbəsblɪkk]
[ɛ]	Fest/feast [fɛst]	gern/gladly [gɛrn]
[ɛ] [ə]	welken/wither [ˈvɛlkən]	Fremde/strangers [ˈfrɛmdə]
Challenge words	vergebens/vainly [fɛʁˈgeːbəns]	erhebt/raises [ʔɛʁˈheːpt]
[ʊ]	Duft/scent [dʊft]	Turm/tower [tʊrm]
[ʊ] [ə]	gesund/healthy [gəˈzʊnt]	Kunde/lore [ˈkʊndə]
Challenge words	unruhige/restless [ˈʔʊnruːɪgə]	Burgruine/castle ruins [bʊrkruˈinə]
[ɔ]	Horn/horn [hɔrn]	Ort/place [ʔɔrt]
[ɔ] [ə]	tropfen/to drip [ˈtrɔpfən]	sonder/without [ˈzɔndəʁ]
[ɔ] [o]	Orgelton/organ tone [ˈʔɔrgəltoːn]	fortgezogen/pulled away [ˈfɔrtgətsoːgən]
[a]	ganz/whole [gants]	an/to [ʔan]
[a] [ə]	andern/others [ˈʔandəʁn]	Gewand/robe [gəˈvant]
Challenge words	wahrhaft/truthful [ˈvaːrhaft]	Balsam/balsam [ˈbalzaːm]
Open vowels	herunter/down [hɛˈrʊntəʁ]	empfunden/felt [ʔɛmˈpfʊndən]

Double Consonants

Highlighted Sounds	#1	#2
[ʃ]	schon/already [ʃoːn]	schlagen/to strike [ˈʃlaːgən]
[ʃt] [ʃp]	Stunden/hours [ˈʃtʊndən]	Spiel/game [ʃpiːl]
[j]	Jahr/year [jaːɾ]	just/just [jʊst]
[ŋ]	bringen/to bring [ˈbɾɪŋən]	Gesang/chant [gəˈzaŋ]
[nn]	Sonne/sun [ˈzɔnnə]	innern/inside [ˈʔɪnnəʁn]
[ll]	Stelle/place [ˈʃtɛllə]	Wellen/waves [ˈvɛllən]
[mm]	Kummer/grief [ˈkʊmməʁ]	Himmel/sky [ˈhɪmməl]
[tt]	zittert/trembles [ˈtsɪttəʁt]	Matten/mats [ˈmattən]
[ss]	fließen/flow [ˈfliːssən]	saßen/sat [ˈzaːssən]
[kk]	Brocken/boulder [ˈbɾɔkkən]	Schmucke/decorations [ˈʃmʊkkə]
[pp]	klappern/rattle [ˈklappəʁn]	doppelt/double [ˈdɔppəlt]
[ff]	treffe/meet [ˈtɾɛffə]	schaffen/to create [ˈʃaffən]
[ɾɾ]	irre/mad [ˈʔɪɾɾə]	Herren/gentlemen [ˈhɛɾɾən]
Challenge words	Schicksal/fate [ˈʃɪkkzaːl]	Lockenschatten/shade [ˈlɔkkənʃattən]
Challenge words	Sommerruh/summer-rest [ˈzɔmməʁɾuː]	Mitherrscher/co-rulers [ˈmɪthɛɾɾʃəʁ]

Mixed Vowels

Highlighted Sounds	#1	#2
[i:]	ihn/him [ʔiːn]	sie/she [ziː]
[y:]	Süd/south [zyːt]	für/for [fyːʁ]
[y:] [ə]	Güte/kindness [ˈgyːtə]	rühren/to affect [ˈʁyːʁən]
Challenge words	fürwahr/in truth [fyːʁˈvaːʁ]	Gefühle/feelings [gəˈfyːlə]
[ɪ]	wild/wild [vɪlt]	Blitz/lightning [blɪtts]
[ʏ]	dünkt/thinks [dʏŋkt]	hübsch/pretty [hʏpʃ]
[ʏ] [ə]	Müller/miller [ˈmʏlləʁ]	Sünde/sin [ˈzʏndə]
Challenge words	verkündet/announced [fɛʁˈkʏndət]	Entzücken/delight [ʔɛntˈtsʏkkən]
[e:]	nehm/take [neːm]	hebt/lifts [heːpt]
[ø:]	strömt/flows [ʃtʁøːmt]	dröhnt/roars [dʁøːnt]
[ø:] [ə]	Flöte/flute [ˈfløːtə]	spröde/brittle [ˈʃpʁøːdə]
Challenge words	Wasserhöhle/water cave [ˈvassəʁhøːlə]	Tröstung/consolation [ˈtʁøːstʊŋ]
[ɛ]	Geld/money [gɛlt]	Netz/net [nɛtts]
[œ]	lösche/delete [ˈlœʃə]	könnt/can [kœnnt]
[œ]	Hörner/horns [ˈhœɐnəʁ]	Schlösser/locks [ˈʃlœssəʁ]
Challenge words	Schöpfungstagen/creation [ˈʃœpfʊŋstaːgən]	vergönnt/granted [fɛʁˈgœnnt]

Diphthongs, Ich-Laut, Ach-Laut

Highlighted Sounds	#1	#2
[ae]	sein/his [zaen]	weiß/white [vaess]
Challenge words	Blümlein/little flower [ˈblyːmlaen]	Kindlein/little child [ˈkɪntlaen]
[ao]	schaut/looks [ʃaot]	Baum/tree [baom]
Challenge words	glauben/to believe [ˈglaobən]	hinaus/outside [hɪˈnaos]
[ɔø]	Freund/friend [frɔønt]	neu/new [nɔø]
Challenge words	euer/your [ˈʔɔøəʁ]	Säugling/baby [ˈzɔøklɪŋ]
[ax] [aːx]	brach/broke [braːx]	Pracht/splendor [praxt]
[ʊx] [uːx]	Schlucht/ravine [ʃlʊxt]	Buch/book [buːx]
[ɔx] [oːx]	hoch/high [hoːx]	gebrochen/broken [gəˈbrɔxən]
[aox]	auch/also [ʔaox]	tauchen/to dip [ˈtaoxən]
[ɪç]	mich/me [mɪç]	flicht/twists [flɪçt]
Challenge words	endlich/at last [ˈʔɛntlɪç]	ruhig/calmly [ˈruːɪç]
[ɛç]	fechten/to fence [ˈfɛçtən]	Allmächtige/Almighty [ʔallˈmɛçtɪgə]
[aeç]	reich/rich [raeç]	Zeichen/mark [ˈtsaeçən]
Mixed v. + [ç]	Sprüche/sayings [ˈʃpryçə]	Tücher/cloths [ˈtyːçəʁ]
[ɔøç]	leuchten/to shine [ˈlɔøçtən]	däucht/seemed [dɔøçt]

French Pronunciation Guide

IPA	English	French	French Formation
[i]	see [si]	ici [isi]	the tongue arch is far forward; more forward than in English
[e]	chaos ['keɑs]	été [ete]	between the [i] and [ɛ] vowel; not a diphthong as in English
[ɛ]	bell [bɛl]	rêve [ɾɛvə]	placement is more forward than in English
[u]	blue [blu]	jour [ʒuɾ]	forward lip rounding; more rounded than in English
[o]	obey [ʔoˈbɛɪ]	pauvre [povɾə]	forward lip rounding; not a diphthong as in English
[ɔ]	ought [ʔɔt]	aurore [ɔɾɔɾə]	forward lip rounding initiated by the cheek muscles
[a]	sigh (Am) [saɪ]	voilà [vwala]	brighter quality than in English; not a diphthong as in English
[ɑ]	father [ˈfɑðə]	âme [amə]	similar to English [ɑ]
[y]		sûr [syɾ]	[i] tongue arch with [u] lip rounding
[ø]		feu [fø]	[e] tongue arch, [o] lip rounding, and color of [ʊ]
[œ]		seul [sœl]	[ɛ] tongue arch, [ɔ] lip rounding, and color of [ʊ]
[ɾ]	thread [θɾɛd]	riche [riʃə]	one flip of the tongue tip against the upper front teeth
[ʃ]	shine [ʃaɪn]	chant [ʃã]	voiceless sibilant
[ʒ]	azure [ˈæʒə]	jamais [ʒamɛ]	voiced sibilant
[ɲ]		vigne [viɲə]	[j] formation with nasalized manner of articulation
[j]	young [jʌŋ]	yeux [jø]	a rapidly enunciated [i]
[ɥ]		nuit [nɥi]	a rapidly enunciated [y]
[d][n][t][l]	dental [ˈdɛntəl]	dentelle [dãtɛlə]	the tongue tip contacts the upper front teeth in French
[b][d][g]	bag [bæg]	vagabonde [vagabõdə]	fully voice without aspiration in French
[p][t][k]	kept [kɛpt]	spectacle [spɛktaklə]	articulate without aspiration in French

French Diction: Week 14

Day 1: Introduction to French Diction

Day 2: Dentals, Plosives, [i], [e], [a], and [w]

Day 3: The [j] Glide, [ɛ] and [ɛ̃]

Day 4: The Back Vowels, [ɑ], [ʃ], [ʒ], and [ɲ]

Day 5: The [ɥ] Glide and [y]

Day 6: The Schwa [ə], [ø], and [œ]

Lesson Notes, Date: _____________

Checklist of Concepts to Review

BREATH
Breath Control___
p: 35, 63, 67
Breath Support___
p: 63, 65
Breath Expansion___
p: 33, 35
DICTION
Articulation___
p: 121, 123, 125, 131
Front Vowels___
p: 57, 105
Back Vowels___
p: 73, 107
Central Vowels___
p: 89, 91, 93, 109, 111
Mixed Vowels___
p: 113, 115
FLEXIBILITY
Flexibility___
p: 109, 139
MUSICIANSHIP
Artistry___
p: 141
Dynamics___
p: 143
Legato___
p: 49, 59, 75, 139, 141

POSTURE
Postural Alignment___
p: 25, 27
RANGE
Range___
p: 81, 91, 139
TONE
Chiaroscuro___
p: 97, 113, 115
Lip Trills___
p: 41, 43
Palatal Resonance___
p: 89, 91, 93, 109
Pharyngeal Space___
p: 57, 59, 93, 105, 109
Projection___
p: 73, 75, 93, 107
Register___
p: 43, 83
Resonance___
p: 93, 95, 97, 109, 137
Sensory Awareness___
p: 61, 127
Vibrato___
p: 43, 45, 51, 77, 79, 81
Vowel Equalization___
p: 79, 95, 137
WARM-UPS___
p: 200-204

WARNINGS
Breathy Tone___
p: 35, 77, 113, 125, 127
Faulty Formation___
p. 111, 127
Faulty Movement___
p. 45, 47
Faulty Onset___
p: 59, 75, 127
Jaw Tension___
p: 31, 111, 121, 123, 125
Nasal Tone ___
p: 111, 127
Pressed Tone___
p: 35, 41, 43, 83
Spread Tone___
p: 57, 61, 73, 111
Tension___
p: 29, 31, 45, 47, 61
Tongue Impeded Tone__
p: 111, 127
OTHER
Choral Singing___
p: 99
Stage Deportment___
p: 145
Vocal health___
p: 147

Daily Notes and Practice Times

Day 1   Practice Time:_____________

Day 2   Practice Time:_____________

Day 3   Practice Time:_____________

Day 4   Practice Time:_____________

Day 5   Practice Time:_____________

Day 6   Practice Time:_____________

Introduction to French Diction

Attributes of the language. The structure of the French language is optimal for legato singing. The spellings of French words accommodate a regular consonant/vowel flow within the phrase.

Stress in French. The vowel of the stressed syllable in the last word of a phrase is long in French. Avoid a weighted accentuation as is found in English and German. All unstressed syllables are equal in weight and pitch. These qualities enhance the legato of sung French.

The stressed syllable is not indicated in dictionary transcription but it is easy to identify. The final syllable of a word is stressed unless that syllable contains a schwa. The penultimate syllable is stressed in final schwa words.

Vowels. The [œ] schwa is the most frequently occurring vowel sound in French lyrics. Schwas are dropped for speech but extended for singing. Gaining a proper understanding of the schwa is vital in order to achieve an accurate pronunciation and an authentic interpretation of French art song. The schwa is neither weak nor shortened within the vocalic flow. The composer's setting most effectively indicates proper pronunciation of the French schwa for lyric diction.

Dental consonants. The consonants in the word *dental* are articulated with the tongue tip touching the upper front teeth. Dental consonants have no aspiration in the tone. Contrast the following English/French words: *decide/décider* [deside], *table/table* [tablə]

Plosive consonants. Voiced *b, d, g,* and their voiceless counterparts *p, t, k,* are articulated with no aspiration in the tone. Contrast the following English/French words: *beauty/beauté* [bote], *purity/pureté* [pyrəte]

French consonants require a light and quick articulation.

IPA symbols. The phonetic symbols needed for French lyric diction are defined on pages 178 and 188. A free diction listening lab is available on the listening page at www.stmpublishers.com.

Assignment: Record the word lists in the following lessons.

Dentals, Plosives, [i], [e], [a], and [w]

Highlighted Sounds	#1	#2
Dental & Plosives [i]	dit/said [di]	nid/nest [ni]
Dental & Plosives [i] [i]	fini/finished [fini]	Mimi/Mimi [mimi]
Dental & Plosives [e]	thé/tea [te]	blé/wheat [ble]
Dental & Plosives [e] [e]	l'été/the summer [lete]	réglé/settled [ʀegle]
Dental & Plosives [e] [i]	guérir/to heal [geʀiʀ]	zéphyr/zephyr [zefiʀ]
Dental & Plosives [i] [e]	brisé/broken [bʀize]	cité/city [site]
Dental & Plosives [i] [e] Challenge	félicité/bliss [felisite]	divinité/deity [divinite]
Dental & Plosives [a]	par/by [paʀ]	tard/late [taʀ]
Dental & Plosives [wa]	toi/you [twa]	quoi/what [kwa]
Dental & Plosives [a] [a]	canards/ducks [kanaʀ]	natal/native [natal]
Dental & Plosives [a] [i]	tari/dried up [taʀi]	dira/will say [diʀa]
Dental & Plosives [a] [e]	garder/to keep [gaʀde]	braver/to brave [bʀave]
Dental & Plosives [a] [i] Challenge	s'abattit/descended [sabati]	Alguazils/Alguacils [algazil]
Dental & Plosives [a/i/e] Challenge	fatigué/tired [fatige]	palpiter/to beat [palpite]
Dental & Plosives [a/i/e] Challenge	nativité/nativity [nativite]	inanimé/unconscious [inanime]

Phrases:

the vivid clarity
la clarté vive
[la klaʀte viv]

guided by friendship,
guidé par l'amitié
[gide paʀ lamitje]

The [j] Glide, [ɛ] and [ɛ]

Highlighted Sounds	#1	#2
[ɛ]	mer/sea [mɛɾ]	vers/towards [vɛɾ]
[ɛ] [a]	avec/with [avɛk]	laissa/left [lɛsa]
[ɛ] [i]	exil/exile [ɛgzil]	permis/permit [pɛrmi]
[ɛ] [e]	bercé/rocked [bɛɾse]	désert/desert [dezɛɾ]
[ɛ] [a] Challenge	asservie/enslaved [asɛɾvi]	fraternité/fraternity [fratɛɾnite]
[ɛ] [i] [e]	destiné/intended for [dɛstine]	servirai/I will serve [sɛɾviɾe]
[jɛ] [je]	hier/yesterday [jɛɾ]	miel/honey [mjɛl]
Medial [j]	voyez/see [vwaje]	briller/to shine [bɾije]
Final [j]	pareil/same [paɾɛj]	réveil/waking up [ɾevɛj]
[ɇ]	les/the [lɇ]	très/very [tɾɇ]
[i] [ɇ]	dirait/he would say [diɾɇ]	discret/discrete [diskɾɇ]
[a] [ɇ]	fallait/had to [falɇ]	palais/palace [palɇ]
[ɛ] [ɇ]	taisais/kept quiet [tɛzɇ]	mettrais/will put [mɛtɾɇ]
[e] [ɇ]	répétait/repeated [ɾepetɇ]	rénaît/reborn [ɾenɇ]

Phrases:

attracting the bees
Attiraient les abeilles
[atiɾe lez abɛj]

if my verses had wings,
Si mes vers avaient des ailes,
[si me vɛrz ave dez ɛlə]

The Back Vowels, [ɑ], [ʃ], [ʒ], and [ɲ]

Highlighted Sounds	#1	#2
[u]	bout/end [bu]	fou/crazy [fu]
polysyllables [u]	courir/to run [kurir]	goûter/to taste [gute]
[o]	trop/too much [tro]	au/to the [o]
polysyllables [o]	vaisseau/ship [vɛso]	poser/to ask [poze]
polysyllables [u o]	fourneau/furnace [furno]	couteau/knife [kuto]
[ɔ]	port/port [pɔr]	vol/flight [vɔl]
polysyllables [ɔ]	donner/to give [dɔne]	alors/then [alɔr]
polysyllables [o ɔ]	locaux/local [lɔko]	taureau/bull [tɔro]
[ɑ]	mâts/masts [mɑ]	las/weary [lɑ]
[a]	clac/slam [klak]	plat/flat [pla]
[ɑ]	passer/to pass [pɑse]	hautbois/oboe [obwɑ]
[ʒ]	bourgeois/bourgeois [burʒwa]	jaunis/yellowed [ʒoni]
[ʃ]	chameau/camel [ʃamo]	toucher/to touch [tuʃe]
[ɲ]	signal/signal [siɲal]	gagner/to win [gaɲe]

Phrases:

There, all is order and beauty
Là, tout n'est qu'ordre et beauté,
[la tu nɛ kɔrdr e bote]

Our love is an eternal thing,
Notre amour est chose éternelle,
[nɔtr amur ɛ ʃoz etɛrnɛl]

The [ɥ] Glide and [y]

Highlighted Sounds	#1	#2
[i]	dis/say [di]	lys/lily [lis]
[i]→[y]	tu/you [ti → ty]	fut/was [fi → fy]
[u]	loups/wolves [lu]	cou/neck [ku]
[u] [y]	courut/ran [kuɾy]	goulu/gluttonous [guly]
2 syllables [y]	jusqu'à/to, until [ʒyska]	vertu/virtue [vɛɾty]
3+ syllables [y]	humanité/humanity [ymanite]	murmurer/to whisper [myɾmyɾe]
[y] [i]	unie/united [yni]	subir/to suffer [sybiɾ]
[j]→[ɥ]	bruit/noise [bɾji → bɾɥi]	suis/am [sji → sɥi]
2+ syllables [ɥi]/[ɥe]/[ɥɛ]	spirituel/spiritual [spiɾitɥɛl]	diminuer/to diminish [diminɥe]
[ɥ] [u]	poursuivez/continue [puɾsɥive]	aujourd'hui/today [oʒuɾdɥi]
2 syllables [ɥ]	réduit/reduced [ɾedɥi]	appui/support [apɥi]
3 syllables [ɥ]	cuirassés/battleships [kɥiɾase]	produira/will produce [pɾɔdɥiɾa]
[w]	soirs/evenings [swaɾ]	dois/have to [dwa]
[j]	fierté/pride [fjɛɾte]	guerriers/warriors [gɛɾje]

Phrases:

over poetry and beauty.
Sur la poésie et sur la beauté.
[syɾ la pɔezi e syɾ la bote]

and you will tell it a ballad
Et lui diras une ballade
[e lɥi diɾaz ynə baladə]

The Schwa [ə], [ø], and [œ]

Highlighted Sounds	#1	#2
[e]→[ø]	veux/want [ve ⟶ vø]	pleut/rains [ple → plø]
[jø]	Dieu/God [djø]	cieux/heaven [sjø]
2 syllables [ø]	glorieux/glorious [glɔrjø]	radieux/radiant [radjø]
3 syllables [ø]	harmonieux/harmonious [armɔnjø]	amoureux/in love [amurø]
[ø] [y]	brumeux/misty [brymø]	juteux/juicy [ʒytø]
[ɛ]→[œ]	cœur/heart [kɛr → kœr]	œil/eye [ɛj → œj]
2 syllables [œ]	meunier/miller [mœnje]	fleuri/flowery [flœri]
Final [œr]	honneur/honor [ɔnœr]	douceur/sweetness [dusœr]
[œr] [y]	pudeur/modesty [pydœr]	rumeur/rumor [rymœr]
3 syllables [œ]	supérieur/superior [syperjœr]	laboureur/plowman [laburœr]
[ə]	le/the [lə]	ce/that [sə]
[œ] [ə]	veuve/widow [vœvə]	peuple/people [pœplə]
2 syllables [ə]	âme/soul [amə]	belle/beautiful [bɛlə]
3 syllables [ə]	tristesse/sadness [tristɛsə]	aurore/dawn [ɔrɔrə]
[ə] [ə]	chevelure/hair [ʃəvəlyrə]	venue/coming [vənyə]

Phrases:

Their short jackets of silk,
Leurs courtes vestes de soie,
[lœr kurtə vɛstə də swa]

farewell, handsome stranger! Alas!
Adieu, beau voyageur! Hélas! Adieu!
[adjø bo vwajaʒœr elas adjø]

French Nasal Vowels

IPA	French	Formation
[ã]	vent [vã]	nasalized [ɔ] vowel
[õ]	monde [mõdə]	nasalized [o] vowel
[ɛ̃]	saint [sɛ̃]	nasalized [ɛ] with [ʌ] color
[œ̃]	un [œ̃]	nasalized [ɛ] with [ɔ] lip and [ʊ] color

Latin Pronunciation Guide

IPA	English	Latin	Latin Formation
[i]	see [si]	mitis ['mitis]	the tongue arch is far forward; more forward than in English
[ɛ]	bell [bɛl]	miserere [mizɛ'rɛɾɛ]	more forward than in English
[u]	dew [dju]	numerus ['numɛrus]	forward lip rounding; more rounded than in English
[ɔ]	ought [ʔɔt]	oculos ['ɔkulɔs]	forward lip rounding initiated by the cheek muscles
[ɑ]	father ['fɑðə]	amara [ɑ'mɑɾɑ]	similar to English [ɑ]
[ɾ]	thread [θrɛd]	propter ['prɔptɛr]	one flip of the tongue tip against the upper front teeth
[r]		rubet ['rubɛt]	articulate a fully voiced rolled "r" with the tongue tip
[ʃ]	shoe [ʃu]	ascendat [ɑ'ʃɛndɑt]	voiceless sibilant [ʃ]
[tʃ]	child [tʃaɪld]	cymbalis ['tʃimbalis]	articulate two voiceless consonants
[dʒ]	judge [dʒʌdʒ]	agens ['adʒɛnz]	articulate two voiced consonants
[ɲ]		regnum ['rɛɲum]	[j] tongue position with a nasal manner of articulation
[j]	young [jʌŋ]	jubilate [jubi'latɛ]	a rapidly enunciated [i]
[ŋ]	wing [wɪŋ]	distinguo [dis'tiŋgwɔ]	[g] tongue position with a nasal manner of articulation
[d][n][t][l]	dental ['dɛntəl]	dentale [dɛn'talɛ]	the tongue tip contacts the upper front teeth in Latin
[b][d][g] [p][t][k]	table ['tɛɪbəl]	pater ['patɛr]	articulate without aspiration in Latin

French, Latin, and English Diction: Week 15

Day 1: Nasals [ã] and [õ]

Day 2: Nasals [ɛ̃] and [œ̃]

Day 3: Introduction to Latin Diction

Day 4: Vowels: [ɛ] and [ɔ]

Day 5: Vowels: [i], [u] and [ɑ]

Day 6: English – Linking within the Phrase

Lesson Notes, Date: ___________

Checklist of Concepts to Review

BREATH
Breath Control___
p: 35, 63, 67
Breath Support___
p: 63, 65
Breath Expansion___
p: 33, 35
DICTION
Articulation___
p: 121, 123, 125, 131
Front Vowels___
p: 57, 105
Back Vowels___
p: 73, 107
Central Vowels___
p: 89, 91, 93, 109, 111
Mixed Vowels___
p: 113, 115
FLEXIBILITY
Flexibility___
p: 109, 139
MUSICIANSHIP
Artistry___
p: 141
Dynamics___
p: 143
Legato___
p: 49, 59, 75, 139, 141

POSTURE
Postural Alignment___
p: 25, 27
RANGE
Range___
p: 81, 91, 139
TONE
Chiaroscuro___
p: 97, 113, 115
Lip Trills___
p: 41, 43
Palatal Resonance___
p: 89, 91, 93, 109
Pharyngeal Space___
p: 57, 59, 93, 105, 109
Projection___
p: 73, 75, 93, 107
Register___
p: 43, 83
Resonance___
p: 93, 95, 97, 109, 137
Sensory Awareness___
p: 61, 127
Vibrato___
p: 43, 45, 51, 77, 79, 81
Vowel Equalization___
p: 79, 95, 137
WARM-UPS___
p: 200-204

WARNINGS
Breathy Tone___
p: 35, 77, 113, 125, 127
Faulty Formation___
p. 111, 127
Faulty Movement___
p. 45, 47
Faulty Onset___
p: 59, 75, 127
Jaw Tension___
p: 31, 111, 121, 123, 125
Nasal Tone ___
p: 111, 127
Pressed Tone___
p: 35, 41, 43, 83
Spread Tone___
p: 57, 61, 73, 111
Tension___
p: 29, 31, 45, 47, 61
Tongue Impeded Tone___
p: 111, 127
OTHER
Choral Singing___
p: 99
Stage Deportment___
p: 145
Vocal health___
p: 147

Daily Notes and Practice Times

Day 1   Practice Time:__________

Day 2   Practice Time:__________

Day 3   Practice Time:__________

Day 4   Practice Time:__________

Day 5   Practice Time:__________

Day 6   Practice Time:__________

Nasals [ã] and [õ]

Highlighted Sounds	#1	#2
[ɔ]	dort/sleeps [dɔɾ]	fort/strong [fɔɾ]
[ɔ]→[ã]	rend/gives back [ɾɔ → ɾã]	chant/song [ʃɔ → ʃã]
[ã] [ã]	penchant/inclination [pãʃã]	dansant/dancing [dãsã]
[ã] [ə]	entre/in between [ãtɾə]	branches/branches [bɾãʃə]
2 Syllables [ã]	voyant/seeing [vwajã]	comment/how [kɔmã]
3 Syllables [ã]	balance/scale [balãsə]	silence/silence [silãsə]
[o]	mots/words [mo]	vaut/worth [vo]
[o]→[õ]	pont/bridge [po → põ]	l'on/that we [lo → lõ]
[õ] [õ]	fondons/we found [fõdõ]	rompons/we break [ɾõpõ]
[õ] [ə]	sombre/dark [sõbɾə]	blonde/blonde [blõdə]
2 Syllables [õ]	rayon/ray [ɾɛjõ]	maison/house [m(e)zõ]
3 Syllables [õ]	colombe/dove [kɔlõbə]	triomphe/triumph [tɾijõfə]
[ã] [õ]	chanson/song [ʃãsõ]	comprend/includes [kõpɾã]
Challenge words [ã] [õ]	nonchalante/nonchalant [nõʃalãtə]	promptement/promptly [pɾõptəmã]

Phrases:

to fall into infinity,
De tomber dans l'immensité,
[də tõbe dã limmãsite]

reward me for my patience!
Me récompensent de l'attente!
[mə ɾekõpãsə də latãtə]

Nasals [ɛ̃] and [œ̃]

Highlighted Sounds	#1	#2
Formation [ɛ]	sert/serves [sɛɾ]	bref/brief [bɾɛf]
Color of: [ʌ]	such [sʌtʃ]	bud [bʌd]
[ɛ]→[ɛ̃]	saint/saint [sɛ → sɛ̃]	bien/good [bjɛ → bjɛ̃]
[ɛ̃ ə]	timbres/tones [tɛ̃bɾə]	demain/tomorrow [dəmɛ̃]
2 syllables [ɛ̃]	jardins/gardens [ʒaɾdɛ̃]	ainsi/thus [ɛ̃si]
[ɛ̃ ɛ̃]	incertain/uncertain [ɛ̃sɛɾtɛ̃]	maringouins/mosquitoes [maɾɛ̃gwɛ̃]
[ã ɛ̃]	enfin/finally [ãfɛ̃]	Saint-Jean/Saint-Jean [sɛ̃ʒã]
[õ ɛ̃]	combien/how many [kõbjɛ̃]	poinçon/punch [pwɛ̃sõ]
Challenge words [ɛ̃]	malandrins/bandits [malãdɾɛ̃]	instrument/instrument [ɛ̃stɾymã]
Formation [œ]	cœur/heart [kœɾ]	deuil/mourning [dœj]
Color of: [ʊ]	cook [kʊk]	took [tʊk]
[œ]→[œ̃]	qu'un/that one [kœ → kœ̃]	uns/the ones [œ → œ̃]
2 syllables [œ̃]	aucun/none [okœ̃]	lorsqu'un/when one [lɔɾskœ̃]
Challenge words [œ̃]	emprunté/borrowed [ãpɾœ̃te]	triumphant/triumphant [tɾijœ̃fã]
[œ̃ ɛ̃]	un prince/a prince [œ̃ pɾɛ̃sə]	un singe/a monkey [œ̃ sɛ̃ʒə]

Phrases:

A sweet, noble agreement:	*mingling a hint of jasmine*
Un doux accord patricien:	Melant un esprit de jasmin
[œ̃ duz akɔɾ patɾisiɛ̃]	[mɛlãt œ̃n ɛspɾi də ʒasmɛ̃]

Introduction to Latin Diction

Attributes of the language. The consonant/vowel flow of the Latin language favors an Italian manner of articulation. Post-classical Latin is a Romance language and its usage in choral settings originates with, and is centered around, the Roman Catholic Church.

Stress in Latin. Articulation of the stressed syllable is weighted in Latin. An advanced understanding of the structure of the language is required in order to determine vowel length and pitch of stressed and unstressed syllables.

Vowels. The formation of Latin vowels is similar to that of the Romance languages. Do not weaken the quality of vowels in unstressed syllables. Avoid a medial placement of the vowel as is heard in English. There are no glottal stops in Latin.

The *au* spelling is pronounced as a falling diphthong. Rising diphthongs occur with intervocalic *i* and *j* spellings, *qu* spelling, and with prevocalic initial *i* or *j* spellings. Other vowel clusters are in hiatus (each vowel occupies a separate syllable). The word *triumph* is an example of an English word with vowels in hiatus.

Dental consonants. The consonants in the word *dental* are articulated with the tongue tip touching the upper front teeth. Dental consonants have no aspiration in the tone. Contrast the following English/Latin words: *defend/defendat* [dɛˈfɛndɑt], *spiritual/spiritalis* [spiɾiˈtɑlis]

Plosive consonants. Voiced *b, d, g,* and their voiceless counterparts *p, t, k,* are articulated with no aspiration in the tone. Contrast the following words: *protect/protegat* [ˈprɔtɛgɑt], *invoke/invocabo* [invɔˈkɑbɔ]

Latin consonants require a light and quick articulation.

IPA symbols. The phonetic symbols needed for Latin lyric diction are defined on page 188.

Assignment: Record the word lists in the following lessons.

Vowels: [i], [u] and [ɑ]

Highlighted Sounds	#1	#2
Dental [n] [ɑ] [i]	animas/souls [ˈɑnimɑs]	sana/right [ˈsɑnɑ]
Dental [l] [ɑ] [i] [u]	laus/praise [lɑus]	filius/son [ˈfilius]
Dental [d] [ɑ] [i] [u]	mundi/world [ˈmundi]	audiam/I will listen [ˈɑudiɑm]
Dental [t] [ɑ] [i] [u]	humilitatis/lowness [umiliˈtatis]	tantum/only [ˈtɑntum]
Dental [ɾ] [ɑ] [i] [u]	futurus/future [fuˈtuɾus]	salutari/to be saved [saluˈtaɾi]
Plosive [k] [ɑ] [u]	adhuc/still [ˈɑduk]	factus/having become [ˈfɑktus]
Plosive [p] [ɑ] [i] [u]	primis/first [ˈpɾimis]	paradisum/paradise [pɑɾɑˈdizum]
Plosive [g] [ɑ] [i] [u]	sanguis/blood [ˈsɑŋgwis]	crucifixus/crucified [kɾutʃiˈfiksus]
Plosive [b] [ɑ] [i] [u]	brachium/arm [ˈbɾɑkium]	habitavit/he dwelt [ɑbiˈtɑvit]
Prepalatal [ɲ] [ɑ] [i]	maligna/malignant [mɑˈliɲɑ]	ignis/fire [ˈiɲis]
Prepalatal [tʃ] [i] [u]	inimici/enemies [iniˈmitʃi]	lucis/light [ˈlutʃis]
Prepalatal [dʒ] [ʃ] [ɑ] [i] [u]	digitus/finger [ˈdidʒitus]	suscipiat/he undertakes [ˈsuʃipiɑt]
[w] Glide [ɑ] [i] [u]	quidquid/whatever [ˈkwidkwid]	numquam/never [ˈnumkwɑm]
[j] Glide [i] [u]	justis/just [ˈjustis]	cujus/whose [ˈkujus]
Double Consonants [ɑ] [i]	affligit/he afflicts [ɑfˈflidʒit]	altissimi/highest [ɑlˈtissimi]

Phrase:

I will sing to thee with the harp, thou holy one of Israel. Psalms 71:22
psallam tibi in cithara, sanctus Israël.
[ˈpsɑllɑm ˈtibi in tʃiˈtɑɾɑ ˈsɑŋktus ˈisɾɑɛl]

Vowels: [ɛ] and [ɔ]

Highlighted Sounds	#1	#2
Initial Vowel [ɑ] [ɛ]	amen/amen ['amɛn]	eja/behold ['ɛjɑ]
Dental [t] [ɛ] [ɔ] [u]	memento/remember [mɛ'mɛntɔ]	votum/vow ['vɔtum]
Dental [l] [ɑ] [ɛ] [i] [u]	elevatis/you lift [ɛlɛ'vatis]	lumine/light ['luminɛ]
Dental [d] [ɛ] [ɔ] [i]	hodie/today ['ɔdiɛ]	Deo/God ['dɛɔ]
Dental [ɾ] [ɑ] [ɔ] [u]	dolor/grief ['dɔlɔɾ]	adoramus/we worship [adɔ'ɾamus]
Plosive [p] [ɑ] [ɛ] [ɔ] [u]	perpetua/perpetual [pɛɾ'pɛtuɑ]	propter/on account of ['prɔptɛɾ]
Plosive [g] [ɑ] [ɛ] [ɔ] [i] [u]	gloria/glory ['glɔɾiɑ]	exaudi/listen [ɛgz'ɑudi]
Plosive [k] [ɑ] [ɛ] [ɔ] [i] [u]	excelsis/highest [ɛk'ʃɛlsis]	custodiat/he guards [kus'tɔdiat]
Plosive [b] [ɑ] [ɛ] [ɔ] [i]	oblationem/offering [ɔblatsi'ɔnɛm]	debita/debts ['dɛbita]
Initial r [ɑ] [ɛ] [ɔ] [u]	reus/defendant ['rɛus]	recordare/remember [rɛkɔɾ'daɾɛ]
Prepalatal [ɲ] [ɑ] [ɛ] [i]	ignem/fire ['iɲɛm]	regnat/he rules ['rɛɲat]
Velar [ŋ] [ɑ] [ɔ] [i] [u]	sanctos/saints ['saŋktɔs]	unctio/anointing ['uŋktsiɔ]
Double Consonants [ɑ] [ɛ] [ɔ] [i]	hosanna/hosanna [ɔ'zannɑ]	confessione/confession [kɔnfɛssi'ɔnɛ]
Double Consonants [ɑ] [ɛ] [ɔ] [i] [u]	attendite/listen [at'tɛnditɛ]	occurrite/meet [ɔk'kurritɛ]

Phrase:

All kingdoms of the earth, sing unto God; Psalms 67:33
Regna terræ, cantate Deo;
['rɛɲɑ 'tɛrɾɛ kan'tatɛ 'dɛɔ]

English – Linking Within the Phrase

IDENTICAL CONSONANT SOUNDS

Elongate identical consonant sounds of separate words unless a stop is involved (*b, d, g, p, t, k*). Rearticulate a stop only if the words are stressed within the phrase or in a slow tempo. Intone the following:

1. Let's sing and cheer our hearts tonight.
2. A low wind sighs thru ghostly trees.
3. A leaf from a wild, white flower,
4. Since I am myself my own fever and pain.
5. And the little brown nightingale bills his best,
6. Through the round window above, the deep palpable blue,
7. But of wisdom, no clock can measure.
8. I did not take her by the hand
9. The dreary woods that bound th'extensive view,
10. I dream her rich cheek rests against my lip.
11. The night puts stars into her hair.
12. Sinking down into the lush shade
13. During sad days, when to me nothing mattered.
14. Made the spring bloom and did the groves inspire;
15. The fog grows heavy on the dew laiden field
16. A message just for me and you.
17. I shall lift up mine eyes to the hills from whence cometh my help.
18. The lazy hum of the busy bees, Murmureth through the almond trees;

VOICED AND VOICELESS COUNTERPARTS

Consonants that share the same formation should be rearticulated. Exception: drop the final *th* of *with* when followed by an initial *th* word. Intone the following:

1. Methinks I could from sleep be free.
2. Charm'd with the magic of her tongue,
3. Beneath this lime tree's fragrant shade,
4. The solemn hour of midnight, Breathes sweetly everywhere.
5. Unto which joys for us to attain,
6. Dim, through the misty panes and thick green light,

WHEN TO AVOID LINKING

A light break is needed if linking would distort the meaning of the text. Look for initial vowel words and indicate what these phrases could imply if the light glottal stop were omitted.

1. And so deceive his jealous eye.

2. And hid from any passing.

3. And with thy ears consider my calling,

4. Now hark, all you gallants! Your ears I would tease

5. The world with all its cares, and I in pain

6. Allow this aged man his right

7. In safety lighted her round the green isle;

8. That seem to shoot from other skies.

9. O bend on me thy tender eyes,

10. And ere it dies away, and ere the morning light,

11. I love not hollow cheek or faded eye:

12. Where'er you walk

13. Fairest isle, all isles excelling,

14. My tender age in sorrow did beginne;

15. All eyes, as rivers, swell'd, did strangely overflow,

16. While the chaffinch sings on the white orchard bough

17. And sea-blue, sea-deep eyes.

18. Their hearts are aching

Daily Warm-ups

1. SILENT EXERCISES (The jaw is released and tongue tip touches the lower front teeth throughout the exercise)

EXERCISE	PURPOSE	PROCESS	GOAL
1. Tongue push-ups	Train the tongue to work independent of the jaw	Release jaw and alternate between "ah" and tongue vowels: [aiaɪaeaɛa]	Maintain the space of "ah" while fronting the tongue
2. Lip rounds	Train the lips to work independent of the jaw	Release jaw and alternate between "ah" and lip vowels: [auaʊaoaɔa]	Maintain the space of "ah" while rounding the lips
3. Palate lifts	Train the palate to remain high while singing	Alternate between the speech and singing space by raising the palate	Discover a high palate for "ah". Apply to #1 and #2.
4. Belly pop-outs	Train the singer to expand low for each breath without collapsing ribs or sternum	Alternate between inhalation and exhalation using a low-expansion pant and release movement	Maintain a noble stance while expanding low for the breath. The chest stays calm.

2. LEGATO AND VIBRATO EXERCISES

EXERCISE	INSTRUCTION	SEQUENCE	GOAL
5. Introductory legato scale	Do not over-shoot the descent. Avoid a glottal or [h] articulation of the tone.	[ŋ - -] [a - -]	Be aware of onsets and connections between tones
6. Introductory lip trill	Allow the voice to pivot quickly between skips	Lip trills	Discover a seamless transition between the registers
7. Standard lip trill	Explore the tones on and above the 5 and 8	Lip trills	Release the pitches to discover vibrato
8. Vibrato discovery	Maintain spin while moving from [ŋ] to [a]	[ŋ-a ŋ-a ŋ-a ŋ-a ŋ-a]	Discover singing with vibrancy while connecting the consonant to the vowel
9. Advanced legato and vibrato	Sing an intensely spinning [ŋ] tone and maintain the spin into the [a] vowel	[ŋ - - a - -]	Combine legato with vibrato in the vowel space

3. DICTION AND FORMATION EXERCISES

EXERCISE	INSTRUCTION	SEQUENCE	GOAL
10. Tongue arch exercise	Train the tongue to move independent of the jaw	[ŋa ŋa ŋa ŋa ŋa]	Maintain a low jaw position while articulating consonants. Release the tongue base.
11. Front vowel exercise	Release the jaw and form [i] with a forward tongue arch. Do not spread the lips.	[ji] slide [ji - - - -]	Discover space by arching the tongue forward. The tongue sides contact upper molars.
12. Back vowel exercise	Release the jaw and form [u] with a gentle, forward rounding of the lips	[wu] slide [wu - - - -]	Discover projection of the tone with lip rounding that is initiated by the cheek muscles
13. Equalizing the vowels	Maintain consistent vibrancy throughout the vowel changes	[uiu iui uiu iui u] [u i e a o u]	Discover equalized vibrancy and resonance for all vowels
14. Exercise by C. Ware	Lightly articulate the consonant. It is an energetic introduction to the vowel.	[pa pa pa pa pa pa pa]	Manage consonant/vowel flow. Apply this exercise to all consonants: [ba ka da]…
15. Exercise by B. Honn	Train the articulators to move independent of the released position of the jaw	[la be da me ni po tu la be]	Release tongue and lip tension, maintain space, and elongate the vowel

4. BREATH CONTROL AND SUPPORT EXERCISES

EXERCISE	INSTRUCTION	SEQUENCE	GOAL
16. Introductory support drill	Expand low for each breath and support the tone	[si si si]	Discover the low expansion and support needed for singing
17. Support and vibrato drill	Use the support (not placement) of the low note to sing the upper tone	[si si si] [i i i]	Engage support throughout the range
18. The fourth skip	Interrupt interfering tension by bending the knees while singing. Release upper tone.	[i - a]	Connect the whole body to the voice and release the spin of the upper tone
19. Advanced support drill	Expand low for the breath and connect the breath with the tone	[i - i i - i i - i]	Unite tone with breath support
20. Support and range drill	Expand low for the breath and maintain vibrato. Explore [æ] above the staff.	[i - a - - - -]	Connect the tone with support in the upper range

5. FLEXIBILITY AND RANGE EXTENTION EXERCISES

EXERCISE	INSTRUCTION	SEQUENCE
21. Introductory flexibility exercise	Pivot from pitch to pitch in a seamless flow of vibrant sound	[no nu no nu no] ~ G. Bitzas
22. Intermediate flexibility exercise	Legato, flexibility, and vowel equalization are combined. Lilt around the pitches in a seamless flow of vibrant sound.	[no nu no nu no nu no nu] [i a i a i a i a] ~ P. Bitzas
23. The 9-tone scale	Maintain vowel clarity and legato throughout the scale while supporting the tone	[i - - - a - - - -]
24. Flexibility and dynamic control drill	Sing [ti] using a soft head voice vibrato. Crescendo into the G using a support and head voice vibrato mix.	[ti ɾo - - - - - -] ~ G. Bitzas

Bibliography

Bibliography

Adams, David. *A Handbook of Diction for Singers*. New York: Oxford University Press, 1999.

Adler, Kurt. *Phonetics and Diction in Singing*. Minneapolis: University of Minnesota Press, 1967.

Bernac, Pierre. *The Interpretation of French Song*. Praeger Publishers, New York 1970.

Blades-Zeller, Elizabeth. *A Spectrum of Voices*. Lanham, Maryland: The Scarecrow Press, 2003.

Colorni, Evelina. *Singer's Italian*. New York: G. Schirmer, 1970.

Davis, Eileen. *Sing French*. Éclairé Press, Columbus, Ohio, 2003.

Dizionario d'Ortografia e di Pronuncia. B. Migliorini, C. Tagliavini, and P. Fiorelli. Torino: ERI/Edizioni RAI, 1981.

Girard, Denis. *Cassell's French Dictionary*. Macmillan Publishing Co., New York 1981.

Grubb, Thomas. *Singing in French*. Schirmer Books, New York 1979.

Hines, Jerome. *Great Singers on Singing*. Limelight Editions, Pompton Plains, NJ 1984.

Hines, Robert S. *Singer's Manual of Latin Diction and Phonetics*. New York: Schirmer Books, A Division of Macmillan Publishing Co., Inc 1975.

Il Nuovo Zingarelli: Vocabolario della Lingua Italiana di Nicola Zingarelli. 11th Edition; general revision by Miro Dogliotti and Luigi Rosiello. Milano: Zanichelli, 1983.

Janes, Michael, Dora Latiri-Carpenter, and Edwin Carpenter, eds. *Oxford French Dictionary & Grammar* Oxford University Press, Oxford 2001.

Langenscheidt's Wörterbuch. Deutsch-English English-Deutsch, New York: Simon & Schuster Inc., 1993.

Marshall, Madeleine. *The Singer's Manual of English Diction*. G. Schirmer, Inc., New York 1953.

Montgomery, Cheri. *IPA Handbook for Singers*. S.T.M. Publishers, 2015.

Montgomery, Cheri. *Phonetic Readings for Lyric Diction*. S.T.M. Publishers, 2015.

Moriarty, John. *Diction*. Boston: Schirmer Music Co., 1975.

Nitze, William, and Ernest Wilkins. *A Handbook of French Phonetics*. Holt, Rinehart and Winston, Inc., New York 1961.

Bibliography

Odom, William and Benno Schollum. *German for Singers*. Belmont, CA: Thomas Learning, 1997.

PONS Online Dictionary. PONS. N.P, n.d. Web. 09 Dec. 2017. <http://www.pons.eu/>.

Retzlaff, Jonathan and Cheri Montgomery. *Exploring Art Song Lyrics*. New York: Oxford University Press, 2012.

Rice, Robin. *Great Teachers on Great Singing*. Gahanna, Ohio: Inside View Press, 2017.

Robert, Paul. *Le petit Robert* [electronic resource]: de la langue française, Nouvelle édition, Vivendi Universal Interactive Publishing, France 2001.

Ross, WM. T. *Voice Culture and Elocution*. The Baker & Taylor Co., New York 1890.

Siebs, Theodor. *Deutsche Hochsprache*. Berlin: Walter De Gruyter & Co., 1969.

The Latin Vulgate Bible, The Holy Bible in Latin Language with Douay-Rheims English Translation, Vulgate.org. Accessed 12/9/2017.

About the Author

Cheri Montgomery is a member of the voice faculty at the Blair School of Music at Vanderbilt University where she has taught voice and diction for over 15 years. She provides postgraduate instruction to voice teachers, diction instructors, and vocal coaches in her *Lyric Diction Workshop* held each summer at Vanderbilt University.

She has been a guest author for the *Journal of Singing,* presenter at the National Association of Teachers of Singing (NATS) National Conference, and mentor voice teacher and featured presenter for the NATS 2019 Summer Workshop at St. Olaf College. She is author of 12 titles on the topics of voice and diction (S.T.M. Publishers) and co-author of *Exploring Art Song Lyrics* published by Oxford University Press. In her work with Oxford, she provided pronunciation and phonetic symbols (IPA) for more than 750 Italian, German, and French art songs. Her method of transcription is published in the appendix of the Oxford text. Her workbooks have been adopted by major universities across the U.S. and in Canada. Book reviews are available at stmpublishers.com.

Performance credits include solo engagements with the Nashville and Knoxville Symphonies and operatic roles with the Nashville Opera. She was awarded full scholarships for graduate study at the University of Tennessee-Knoxville through the Grace Moore Graduate Scholarship and the Phi Mu Alpha Scholarship, and was a first-place winner of regional NATS auditions. She was also employed as a high school and elementary music teacher, and a classical radio announcer for WUOT, Knoxville.